ISBN-13: 978-1548983444
ISBN-10: 1548983446

Blue Rose Bookstore: the Gift of Why by Karen Barno, published by www.KarenBarno.com.

www.Facebook.com/KarenBarno

© 2017 Karen Barno, First Edition

All rights reserved. No portion of this book may be reproduced in any form without permission from the publisher, except as permitted by U.S. Copyright law. For permission contact Karen@KarenBarno.com.

Visit the author's website at www.KarenBarno.com.

Disclaimer:

This is a work of fiction. Names, characters, businesses, events and incidents are the products of the author's imagination. Any resemblance to actual persons, living or dead, actual locations, or actual events is purely coincidental. If you believe there is any resemblance to you, you may want to look deep within and wonder....WHY?

Introduction

Annie was enjoying her iced tea, feeling the mist blow in off the ocean. The skies were overcast, typical for a June morning. *"June gloom, they call it. Wonder why? Nothing gloomy about taking a walk, listening to the waves lap up on the shoreline, smelling the salt in the air and hearing the sounds of the town waking up. I am blessed."*

Walking past Terri's Coffee and Tea Shop, she noticed a young woman talking loudly into her phone. Annie wasn't sure what she was saying but something about being lost in this "crazy town," which made Annie laugh out loud, and just then the girl on the phone looked over and gave her the middle finger. Annie laughed harder and louder this time and thought, "*She's early.*"

Cassandra-
Here is to you
finding your gift &
why. I'll be take you
where you are suppose to be!

Kari Bass
U.S. 2018

Chapter 1

"That was a wild meeting wasn't it Annie? Intense, but I still think the advisory board provides great advice. What do you think?" Mike Williams, the Advisory Board chair, asked her with a wink.

"I think every time this group gets together it is extremely intense," Annie said, part laughing, part serious, "but you all have offered great advice over the years on my plans to grow my company. If you remember, when we started these meetings, I had two assisted-living communities and now we're up to fifteen. Not bad in a few short years. But as I said in the meeting, I have an aggressive growth plan to build or acquire forty to fifty communities over the next five years."

"I agree…if that is what you really want to do," Mike said walking towards her, "I've always said you must be 100% committed to growing the company. You can't be somewhat committed; it has to be all or nothing. And if you ask my opinion, I'm not sure you *are* all the way in. I feel like you are holding back, still uncertain about the direction you want to take your business and life."

"Mike, stop! We have been over this a million times. I have been all-in since Nick came home twenty years ago and told me about the distressed assisted living community he was helping through bankruptcy. We did our homework and found it to be a growth industry, and knew it was perfect for us. With Nick's legal mind and my business acumen, we're the perfect team. Now with the kids grown they want to be more involved too, so we are all systems go. Plus, Mike, you knew back when you first invested what my goal was. It has always been to grow to about fifty communities, then let Nickolas take over the company. I believe we've been holding at fifteen for way too long."

"I agree that Nickolas has this business in his blood. That's all he has known since birth so of course he has always wanted to be part of it. But do you, Annie? Really?"

Annie was so tired of this line of questioning from Mike; she was not used to anyone questioning her motives or any of her decisions. She had a strong personality and was known for her "don't mess with me" temper. When she was backed into a corner she'd come out swinging and totally demoralize her adversary...then just walk away.

"You know, Mike, it seems like yesterday when we first met, and you asked then if I was all-in. I said yes. Now twenty years later we're still covering this ground. Back then you were just looking to invest the piles of money you made from selling your tech company and you decided to put the money in assisted living. Even then you knew coupling your technology knowledge with healthcare was the future. You saw a huge green light flashing and yes, you bet right."

"No regrets." Mike responded, "Hell, you have made back my investment and more, actually more than I even thought possible in the beginning. But before I invested I made sure it was what I wanted to do! I feel like you haven't stopped to do a needed gut check in a very long time...if ever." Mike stopped to remember his "dark days," as he often referred to them. "Back in the day I was going full tilt, not sleeping, not eating, and drinking every day. I needed a break, and taking that break completely changed my life. And I see you're doing the same, pushing too hard. Annie, the winner is not always the one who has the most chips in the end. Sometimes it's the one who knows when to exit stage right."

"La de da for you, Mike!" Annie responded sharply. "Stop with the bullshit. I'm in fantastic shape and I can out-work and out-hustle those twenty-year-olds, including my son and daughter. And yes, I have a glass of wine or two each night, but I know when to stop. Good grief, Mike I am more focused now than ever on my goals!"

"On your goals, correct. On your family, correct. On *you*, I don't think so. I don't think you ever really stop and smell the roses."

Annie glared at him for a few minutes, then speaking softly, watching her every word, "For your information, after preparing for these advisory meetings, yes, perhaps I get two or three hours of sleep. But to be fair, this is really the only time we see each other anymore, with you constantly traveling. Trust me, the rest of the time it's fine. I sleep fine, I eat fine, I socialize fine...hell, Mike, I have sex fine. Anything else you want to know?"

That cracked Mike up, "Good to know! I'm sure that makes your husband happy." Before Annie could respond, Mike continued. "How many hours do you really sleep a night?" He thought Annie always looked exhausted.

"Well, DAD!!! Six or seven hours is all I need."

But in truth, Annie actually slept closer to two or three hours a night. She had always had trouble sleeping, so an occasional drink helped her. *"No harm, no foul. Never hungover, always up earlier than anyone else, fully prepared, and ready to go."* Alcohol was never a problem and did not interfere in her life. It was something she enjoyed.

"You mean to tell me you get six to seven hours of sleep a night? I hardly believe that one."

"Screw you, Mike."

"Ah, there's that famous Annie edge, and I'm so blessed I got to see it twice in one meeting. I clearly touched a nerve, didn't I, Annie?"

Annie stuttered for a second then regained her composure. "Mike, unlike you who is retired, I have actual work to do. Go bother your staff - you pay them, they have to listen."

"Well, in a way I pay you as well," Mike softly responded.

"OK, you win. I feel like this conversation is leading up to a point. I have a million other things I could be doing, so what do you really want to say?"

"I'll make a deal with you."

"A deal? OK? What?"

"I have a small beach cottage on the coast." Mike chuckled. "Well, when I say on the coast, I mean on the beach. When you step out the patio door your toes are touching sand. I am going to Italy to visit my son for the next couple months. To get to my point, why don't you take time off and get some rest? Think about the expansion plans you want to accomplish in the next two or three years. But you have to go by yourself...no Nick and no Ruth, just you."

"Mike, I don't have...."

Holding up his hand he stopped her, "Annie, I have been exactly where you are right now. Take a break, sit by the water, take time to think, reflect. It will do wonders for your soul. You can take a week."

"Easy for you to relax! Hell, you're an eighty-year-old billionaire. You're accountable to no one except Jan, who happens to be the love of your life. Your kids are grown with children of their own. I'm still in the growth stage, Mike - I don't have time for that nonsense. I'll take time off in a few years after I achieve my goals and am ready to turn over the company to my kids."

"Again, Annie, how much will be enough? And, at what cost? And talking about money, I know for a fact you and Nick are doing extremely well financially. Maybe not billionaires yet, but I know in the high seven figures. Of course having Big Nick for a father-in-law helps, I'm sure."

Annie started to answer. "Wait, wait...was that a smile that almost crossed your face?" Mike said mockingly. "The mention of Big Nick makes you smile? Wow, I'll have to tell him he's on the good list."

"Move on, Mike. The only reason you know he's an investor is because of your personal relationship with him. You know we're a privately held company and keep that information confidential. Listen, I'll know when it's enough. But, let's get back to the deal. You know I love deals, especially involving money." Annie was trying to move the conversation forward. It was growing very uncomfortable and getting a bit too close to home for her.

Mike continued with his proposal, "You have to go stay at my house for at least four days. In return, I will not question your all-in ever again. Plus, I'll give or get you the financing you are looking for to grow at least thirty more communities. Plus...ah, wait...I'll open my Rolodex to you to find the rest."

"Are you serious? You would give me access to the 'Friends of Mike's Billionaire Club'?"

"How did you know about...never mind. I'll never figure out how you know most of what you know. Yes, that list!"

"Deal!" she answered quickly, to wrap up the conversation. "I'll let you know when I can go."

Walking to the door, Mike turned quickly, "No, you'll go soon if you want the financing. Annie, you will love this town. It's a quaint beach town and my favorite place on earth. I will email you the codes to get in the cottage. There is also a full time housekeeper - I'll let her know you will be visiting soon, very soon. Stay there for a few days and then, *only* then, will I keep my end of the deal. But the deal expires in seven days from today so chop chop." Mike yelled closing the door.

"Wait, what's the town called?" Annie yelled after him.

Mike yelled back through the closing door, "The town of Blue Rose...enjoy!"

Annie stood frozen in place. "*Blue Rose, why does that sound familiar to me? I've heard of that somewhere. Where?*"

Then she remembered someone telling her, "All will be well at the Blue Rose."

"Who told me that?"

Chapter 2

Annie was enjoying a glass of 2003 Emidio Pepe Montepulciano d'Abruzzo and reflecting on her conversation with Mike, as she waited for Ruth. Annie and Ruth had been college roommates, so Annie was beyond thrilled when Ruth had agreed to join the company more than twenty years ago. She first agreed to be Annie's personal assistant but then quickly became a business partner and confidant.

It was almost 5:30 p.m. and the hotel lounge was filling up with a mix of vacationers and business people. Annie thought, *"How do people have time to take vacations? I can't remember my last vacation - maybe when our youngest graduated from high school. Has it been that long? Where did the time go?"*

Annie and Ruth always met after the Advisory Board meeting so Ruth could get an update on the outcomes from the meeting, and the women could plan their schedule. Annie wanted to visit the communities she owned and start meeting with possible investors to create some momentum for her growth plans.

One of Ruth's greatest attributes was keeping Annie organized and on time. Everyone who knew Annie knew that she was a talker. When time got away from her, Ruth gently nudged her and she knew to wrap it up. Ruth was always able to say things to Annie that only Nick could also get away with.

Annie was a visionary and often needed to be brought down to reality. Ruth knew better than most that when Annie had a new idea, she believed with all her heart she could accomplish that goal.

Annie was startled by the loud laughter of the group seated at the table next to her. She glanced past the group in time to see Ruth enter the lobby and watched her walk through the lounge. Heads always turned when Ruth walked by; she had been a model in high school and still had the look. Her posture was perfect and she was always perfectly dressed for the occasion. Today Ruth wore a navy blue tailored pantsuit and a bright orange blouse, with perfectly coordinated jewelry. Her long sandy blonde was cut perfectly to her face shape, and never was anything out of place. *"She looks the same today as when we met in college,"* Annie thought.

"Where have you been? I've been waiting forever for you." Annie asked with a touch of frustration in her voice. "We have much to do."

"Obviously you didn't mind waiting, considering you're on your second glass of wine." Ruth quickly snapped back. "Isn't it a bit early?"

"You too?" Annie shot back. "Mike has been busting my chops about this as well. Can we just get focused on the important stuff? Give me the damn financials so we can determine which communities to visit first."

Ruth opened her briefcase and started to pull out the file. She always made sure financials were on top because Annie always wanted them first regardless of what the meeting was about.

Annie snapped her fingers and said loudly and impatiently, "Can you hurry the hell up? Come on, there is no need to move at a snail's pace."

"Here is the file." Ruth tossed it onto the table, giving Annie an icy stare.

Annie looked up at Ruth, realizing that she was being rude. "I am sorry, Ruth - I'm just on edge from the meeting with the board and need to wind down." Annie gestured to the waiter. "Trevor, another glass of wine, please?"

"Annie," Ruth said leaning in. "I've known you longer than your husband has. If you remember, I introduced the two of you."

"Yeah, yeah, how can I forget? You remind me all the time!" Annie faked exasperation.

Before replying, Ruth took a few seconds to make sure she framed her words correctly. She didn't want to see an Annie explosion in a crowded bar. "OK, I say this with love in my heart. Take some damn time off. You are exhausted. You don't sleep, you're drinking more and more, you work non-stop and barely make time to catch your breath. Yes, I know, you have been like this your entire life, but if you don't slow down and take a break the universe will slow you down. Look what happened to Nick."

Annie thought back to that incident three years ago. It actually seemed like just yesterday when Nick had collapsed with a heart attack while presenting at a conference. Annie was so scared. Nick was the yin to her yang. He was her guy and she was his girl. They truly completed each other and had a marriage that most who knew them envied.

Annie and Nick had clicked the first night they met at a library, and were inseparable from that moment on.

Nick graduated a year before Annie and started his own law firm. His father, "Big Nick," had wanted Nick to join his large, powerful, politically active law firm "to the Hollywood and political elite," as it was called. But Nick wanted to follow his own path. He and Annie discussed their options for a long time and decided to go it alone. They both were confident in his abilities, and once Big Nick got over his decision to not join the firm, he gently coaxed business over Nick's way. Nick and Annie were forever grateful to Big Nick for helping them out. They understood how hurt he had been, but he had grown to accept it.

The couple were married in September, five months after Annie's graduation. It was considered the must-attend wedding event of the year. They married at Nick's family's Catholic church, with the reception at the Hermitage Country Club. This country club was known as the place for all the Hollywood elite to rub elbows with the who's who of senators, governors and lobbyists. The media coverage was out of control and people were begging to be invited. There seemed to be more secret service agents and private security than attendees at the wedding.

"Doesn't she look stunning?" Julia said as she glanced over at her husband, Ruth's father, the two-time elected sitting Governor of the State.

"She does indeed. That dress is a perfect fit. You had a hand in picking that out, my dear?" the Governor asked the First Lady in a quizzical manner.

"I did, but she paid for it."

"Come on, Julia, I know where you and Ruth took her shopping."

With a sly grin Julia said, "Well, we may have 'encouraged' the sales person to knock off $21,000. Annie proudly paid $1200 for the dress."

"And you, my dear?" the Governor asked, crossing his arms and pretending to be angry.

"Does that matter, dear? What's money if you can't enjoy it and do good with it?" Distracting him, Julia quickly said, "I think this is the happiest I have ever seen her."

"That girl scares me, Julia. I told you that on the first day we met her," the Governor whispered to the First Lady.

"Me too." Big Nick said as he walked up and joined the conversation. "Me too, Governor. Hello, Madam First Lady."

"Stop it, both of you." Julia said sternly, "She will be just fine. If there is one thing I know for sure about that young lady, she's determined."

The First Lady looked over just as Annie's mother approached the group. "Hello, Mrs. Thompson."

"Hello, First Lady, Governor," and then Mrs. Thompson curtsied.

"Oh please, stop it, call us Julia and the Governor." Everyone cracked up except Annie's mother, who didn't understand. She was a fish out of water in that group and, well, truly the whole wedding.

"Your daughter looks positively radiant." The Governor said to Mrs. Thompson.

"She does," Annie's mother said, beaming with pride.

At the head table, Brad, the best man and Ruth's fiancée, stood up, clinked the wine glass imported from Italy with his spoon, cleared his throat and announced, "It's time for the toast!"

Upon hearing Brad's announcement, Annie's mother said, "Please excuse me. I need to be with my daughter."

Julia waited until Mrs. Thompson was far enough away and said in a low tone, "Bitch."

"Julia, First Ladies do not talk like that." The Governor said, chuckling.

"This First Lady does, and she *is* a bitch! Look at her, acting like the greatest mother ever. Never mind, I have got to let it go!"

After Brad's toast Annie took a sip of her wine and set the glass down. The waiter started to refill her glass but Annie stopped him, as she had made a decision before the wedding to have wine only at the toast. She wanted to make sure to be in total control, especially with all the press walking around.

Big Nick looked at the Governor and First Lady and cleared his throat, "You know, Julia, Annie has just been handed the keys to the kingdom and that scares the fuck out of me. Excuse me, the crap out of me."

The Governor laughed out loud, saying to Big Nick, "No need to change that word, Nick, I completely agree with you."

"Both of you, stop it now!" Julia was angry. "As I said over and over to you both, there is one thing I know beyond a shadow of a doubt about Annie: I would never, ever bet against her. She has a fire that burns within that will make sure she accomplishes all her dreams. And she loves Nick more than anything, so trust me no person will ever split them up."

As if she had heard what Julia said, at that moment Annie looked across the room directly at her and thought, "I like holding the keys to the kingdom. It gives me hope."

Julia, staring back at Annie, thought to herself, 'Yes, young-un you have this and more. But don't worry, I'm watching over you!"

Annie became distracted and when she looked back over at Julia, she was engaged in another conversation. *"That's odd. Did that just happen ...and what did just happen? Did I just have a long distance 'mental' conversation with Ruth?"* As Annie walked away, she heard *"yes"* in her mind and knew instantly it was Julia answering. *"How awesome is that? Who knew that was really possible? I need to ask her about that next time we meet."*

Following the reception, Annie and Nick set off for their honeymoon in Punta Mita. Returning home, a retirement community owned by one of Nick's clients was looking for someone to work in sales. After interviewing Annie, they knew she would be perfect for the job. Although she accepted the position, she already had her sight set on a loftier goal - to eventually be an owner. That opportunity soon presented itself, and Nick and she purchased their first community. They started a family and had their son, Nick III, who they called Nickolas, and soon after, their daughter Emma. But motherhood never slowed Annie down.

Now grown, both children worked in the family business. Emma was an innovator and loved working on the creative side. Nickolas was the perfect combination of his parents; he loved the elegance of the law but also had the relationship building skills and charisma of his mother. Everyone knew he would be CEO once his mother retired, however, being young, Nickolas was becoming impatient with how slowly Annie was growing the business, as he thought she should be more aggressive in moving the company forward.

Snapping back to reality, Annie finally responded to Ruth's comment about Nick's heart attack. "Ruth, come on now. Nick was fifty pounds overweight, smoked like a chimney and was traveling like a crazy man. We were two ships passing in the night back then. Now look at him. He is fit, slim, and happy with his company. Now he only accepts clients that fit his model. To be honest I think he works probably three days a week and makes four times what he made working full time only a few years ago. It's all good."

"What's the difference between you now and him then?" Ruth wondered out loud.

"Well, I'm not fifty pounds overweight." Annie said exasperated, "Geez, I just had this same conversation with Mike. I'm 5'8', I weigh 127 pounds, and passed my most recent physical with flying colors. I am in amazing shape. Admit it, Ruth...come on, I want to hear you say it. 'Annie you're amazing.' "

In fact, Annie appeared taller than she was, and lean; her clothes always fit her frame perfectly and, like Ruth, everything always matched. Under Ruth's mentorship, she too looked like she had just stepped out of the latest fashion magazine. Understandably, Ruth always thought, considering the years when Annie had nothing at all. When Annie began to make money the first area she focused on was her overall appearance, including clothing.

One thing about Annie that both scared Ruth and that she admired was how quickly Annie could figure people out. Annie could quickly assess what people wanted and how she could help them, while simultaneously achieving her own goals. No one could read people faster than she could, and that's what most contributed to her ability to get along with people. She could diffuse a situation in seconds, or conversely, blow up a situation in the same short amount of time. Her temper, when she believed she was crossed, was legendary in the business.

All of a sudden Annie's thoughts drifted off....

Annie stayed in the other room. He walked in, grabbed her by the hair. "I said to get your ass moving. They want to play cards with you." She just stood there. He walked over, pulled out the belt, whispering in her ear, "Remember what happened last time?" So she sat down to play poker.

"Well," Ruth said, continuing the conversation, "it's 6:30, you've had four glasses of wine and I bet you skipped breakfast. In fact, I'm guessing you really haven't eaten since dinner last night. Now explain to me how in the hell that is taking care of yourself?"

"Screw you, Ruth. If I need a lecture I'll call Mike." Annie picked up her wine glass, slowly emptied it and pointed to the waiter to refill it. "Hey, speaking of Mike, he offered me his beach cottage in return for financing."

"What? Annie, that's amazing!" Ruth continues, "You packed yet? Want my help?"

"I'm not sure I'm going to go. I just don't have time. I did call Nick and he said to go...what do you think?"

Ruth started laughing. "Brad has been begging me to take some time to visit the island and hotel my parents left me. I am sure Nickolas would be thrilled to have you out of his hair for a few days. It would cut his emails by at least 90%." Ruth leaned forward in her chair, pushing her water glass out of the way. "Look, Annie, this will be a great opportunity for you to see if he's ready to be the next CEO. Plus," Ruth continued, laughing, "plus I may have a bet with Nickolas that he'll have to stage a 'palace coup' to get you out of the company."

'Nice, Ruth, real nice! Nickolas would never do that...would he?" Annie asked, with apprehension in her voice. "I'll need to ask him about that one," she said laughing.

The vibrating of Annie's phone interrupted their conversation. "It's from Mike. Must be his codes. Oh no...nice, Mike," Annie said as she read the text to Ruth.

" *'If you want the financing you'll go take a break and think, otherwise I'm out.'* This is bullshit! I hate being beholden to frigging investors. I should tell him to cram his money." The waiter walked over and started to set her glass of wine down. "Excuse me...I've changed my mind. I'll have a martini, straight up, two olives. Well, Ruth, we need his damn money and connections so I don't see that I have a choice."

"Sure you have a choice. That is, if you're not looking for additional financing. Annie, maybe you're happy right where you are. I've told you a thousand times that's OK if you are," Ruth placed her hand on Annie's. "It's your damn company, your blood, sweat and a hell of a lot of tears. I've never asked you, but do you *want* to grow it or not?"

"You sound like Mike." Annie took a deep breath and looked away.

"Hey," Ruth said, wanting to change Annie's mood quickly by planning the trip. "Let's fly there together! We can get some work done on the plane then drop you off. I'll continue on and meet Brad at the island. You know, Annie, I love saying that. How cool...I own an island!"

Ruth slowly sipped her iced tea to give herself a moment to reflect. "You know, Annie, it's still so overwhelming to me that my parents even own a private island. I always thought some wealthy donor owned it and just allowed us to use it. You know what I mean, to gain favor with my father. Clearly I was wrong, and now, it's mine!"

"If you're done going down memory lane, flying together sounds like a plan."

"Plus, as a bonus," Ruth added, "I can make sure you actually get off the plane in...what's the name of the town again?"

"Blue Rose, Ruth...the town of Blue Rose. Four days will be more than enough to fulfill my end of the deal with Mike. Please return on Monday first light to pick me up."

Rolling her eyes at Annie as only Ruth could, "The plane will be there Monday, but the first light is a bit dramatic even for you, darling."

"Maybe so, but stay close to your phone. If something comes up and I need to leave, I want you to be ready on a moment's notice...deal?"

"Oh sure, absolutely." Ruth's voice was dripping with sarcasm, "You do know you're not being held hostage, right? But, if it makes you feel better, deal. Pinky shake. Hey, where's the cottage located, again?"

"I give up," Annie said sipping her martini.

Chapter 3

Annie and Ruth boarded the company plane and walked over to the pilot. "Jake, how long is this damn flight?"

"Good morning, Mrs. Walker and Mrs. Stone. It is two hours and seventeen minutes short." Jake had been Annie's pilot since they bought the plane a few years before.

"Short...short? You are nuts, Jake." Annie yelled. "But hey, feel free to fly slowly."

Shocked by Annie's comment, Jake answered, "You have never said that to me, ever. On each and every flight you say, 'Jake, don't stop for lights.'"

"Come on, Jake, that one is a classic and cracks me up every time I say it." Annie was laughing. "Right, Ruth?"

They put on their lap belts and soon were off. The moment the plane leveled out Annie started snapping her fingers at Ruth for the financials.

Ruth looked over, ignoring her snapping. "Hey, how much should we ask Mike to help us secure?"

"Hmmm, I don't know. I hadn't really had time to think about it."

"You're joking, right? You do know who you're talking to, right? Annie, I know you better than anyone else, I am sure of that...well maybe Nick knows you better, but only because you sleep with him." Ruth stopped in mid-sentence. "...and maybe my mother. Just kidding, I think. Anyway my point is, dear, you sleep, eat and drink money."

"Ruth, wait a minute," Annie said with a mocking tone. "Did you just proposition me? Are you jealous I sleep with Nick? Do you want some of this action? I'm sure you've heard I am really good! Been at it a long time, developed a level of expertise. My, my, Ruth, honey, I don't know what to say. I never saw that in your personality, but hey, maybe after all these years you've decided it's time to walk on the wild side. I'll have to think about it. You know, Ruth, it could be awkward...." Annie leaned back in her chair with a mischievous grin, waiting for Ruth's response.

"Annie, stop it. You know what I meant. Money and you make a wonderful team, great bed partners. And no, I never heard of your bedroom prowess and thank God. Now I need to get the visual out of my head."

Annie stood up and headed over to the galley. "Speaking of wine, let's have a glass." While pouring the wine, she looked over at Ruth and winked.

"Are you changing the subject?"

"Nope, just thirsty. *Now* I'm changing the subject. You know, Ruth, I truly miss your mom. We used to have the best conversations."

"About sex?" Ruth asked with a horrified look. "I don't think my mother and I ever spoke about sex. In fact, you're the first person I had ever met that is so open about the subject."

"Did you know she would visit me at the library when I was working, just to talk? It always seemed like she knew exactly when I was broke because she would show up with lunch. We would eat and talk about anything and everything. You know, in retrospect I'm not sure I was the hardest working employee at the library. Oh well."

"I knew my mother thought of you as a second daughter, and I sort of knew about the lunches. Dad told me that he was sure she visited you more than me."

"That's not true, Ruth...well, at least I don't think so. You, Ruthie, as she called you, were the love of her life. She adored you and was so proud of you even when you decided not to go into the family business. In fact, I always got the vibe that Julia was relieved."

Pausing for a moment, remembering, Annie finally continued, "She gave me the best advice ever."

Ruth looked at Annie with a disbelieving look. "And what advice was that, my friend? Don't wear tennis shoes that have holes in them to an important job interview?"

"Hey now, I loved those tennis shoes. But, no. She stopped by with lunch one day when I was so hung over. Don't bother saying it, I know, what a shock. Seriously, she made the most powerful comment, one I have never forgotten.

"Your mom put her hand on mine, leaned in really close and in a low, motherly voice whispered, 'Annie, the decisions you make today will have a profound effect on your tomorrow.'"

"Interesting," Ruth mumbled.

"Well, daughter of a sitting Governor, for me, not raised in a family whose life was under a microscope, it was." Annie hesitated for a moment, thinking back to college. "After that conversation I stopped that pattern of going to bars and, well, you know."

"I never knew about the conversation but guessed. My mother and I both talked and worried about your proclivity to, ummm, how do I say this...?"

"Ruth, sleep around. Come on girl, you can say it, sleep around. I sowed my wild oats and yours too while I was at it." Annie's voice trailed off....

"You're such a slut. You were born to please me and do what I tell you to do. Doesn't matter where or when I tell you to take off your clothes, you do that. You know why?"

"No," Annie answered weakly.

"Because that's what pigs like you do. Now take off your clothes or I'll get the belt."

"Annie, Annie, earth to Annie!" Ruth said raising her voice to get Annie's attention.

"What?" Annie snapped back to the present. "Sorry, lost my focus, Ruth. Come on, we both know...wow, I guess your mother knew too...I would go to the bar, get drunk, perhaps go home with someone, or not. But did you know I would go home with someone but I never, ever, spent the night? I always went to another friend's house to sleep it off and return to the dorm like nothing happened. But after the conversation with Julia, I was more cautious of my actions, and in fact, met Nick almost right after that."

"My mother knew," Julia quietly responded.

"What? I'm confused. What are you referring to?"

"My mother knew you never spent the night. She found it odd and interesting all at the same time."

That last statement hung in the air as if a dense fog had floated into the cabin of the plane. Annie sat there staring at Ruth, trying to think of something to say. "How? Why? I'm, I'm...I got nothing."

"You know, Annie, there always seem to be people who surround and protect you. Always someone watching you."

"I know, Ruth...don't know how I know or why, but it's true," Annie started staring into space again. "You have never asked, Ruth, but I feel like I need to say that I have never cheated on Nick to this day. I bet that comes as a surprise to you."

"Annie, I never asked, because that would never fit with your personality to cheat on him. You are loyal to the death...well, unless someone crosses you."

They sat in silence for a while, then Annie got up for a second glass of wine. Ruth's head popped up from the file she was reviewing, "Hey, Annie, now that you have decided to do some truth talking, you know what I never asked?"

Annie stopped in mid-pour, and let out a long dramatic sigh. "What can of worms have I opened this time? I just told you I never cheated on Nick - that rules out sleeping with you. Well, would that count? Maybe not!"

"Annie! Stop it!" Ruth was trying to act mad.

"Yes, dear."

"When my mother passed away, how did you know?"

"What do you mean?"

"Annie, you were on the other side of the country at a conference. I hadn't had time to even tell you she was back in the hospital. Yet ten minutes after she passed, you called." Ruth's voice trailed off, as she and Annie got lost in their memories of that night.

"Ruth," Dr. White was trying to get Ruth to listen. The Governor was so focused on his wife that he was unintentionally ignoring the doctor as well. "Ruth...the First Lady."

"You mean my mother!" Ruth said abruptly to Dr. White.

"Yes, Ruth, I'm very sorry." The Doctor had been unsure what the protocol was in this instance. "Your mother's breathing is challenged and I'm not sure it will be much longer. Is there anything you want us... me...to do?"

Ruth stared blankly back at him, "Yes. Discretion. Please, please, please be discreet. Tell our press secretary - I'm sure she's right outside. Ask her to keep the press at bay and away from my dad, please."

Ruth drew in a heavy sigh at the thought of dealing with the press.

"Ruth, this floor is closed off to all nonessential personnel. I have been your family's doctor since before you were born and I promise, no, I guarantee, you will be left alone and no announcement will be made until *your family* chooses to make it."

Ruth started crying but caught herself. She walked back into the room and stood next to the bedside, holding her mom's and dad's hands. At 7:57, the First Lady passed, and Ruth started sobbing uncontrollably, hugging her father.

Annie hesitated, waiting for Ruth to look up, and when she did Annie whispered, "Are you sure you want me to tell you? It's kind of out there, for you."

"Yes."

"Nick and I were staying at that hotel on the ocean." Annie could see Ruth was starting to tear up. "Are you sure this is the time and place to talk about this?"

"Yes, please go on." Ruth almost cracked a smile. "Of course you were at some beach."

"Do you want to hear the story? Because I would much rather talk about my love affair with the ocean."

"Continue."

"I must have fallen asleep on the balcony, and your mom came to me in a dream. At least I think it was a dream. It seemed so real. But it couldn't have been, could it? To this day it seems so real. Anyway, Julia asked that I protect you. To make sure you got rest during that time. 'Ruthie always takes care of everyone else and never herself. Make sure she takes care of herself. Her father will be fine. If he wants to remarry, tell them both I'm fine with that.'"

Ruth interjected, "That will never happen. He still tells me he could never love another woman like he loved mom." Annie looked over and saw tears rolling down her face again.

"You're killing me. Ruth, are you going to stop interrupting?"

"Yes," she said, wiping the tears from her face.

Annie continued with the dream. "Your mother asked that I watch over you, Ruthie. *'Make sure she knows she is deeply loved. She is the best daughter I could have ever asked for. She is the most loving giving person on this planet. Make sure she always knows that she was loved. Promise me, Annie. Promise that if Brad does anything EVER to hurt her you will take care of him.'*"

"Wait," Ruth held up her hand to stop Annie, "that would never happen. Why did she even say that?"

"Ruth!" Annie yelled then continued. "I said, 'Bet your ass. I will bury him and the bones will never be found.'" Annie had to hold up her hand again to stop Ruth. "'But Julia, be assured he adores your daughter and married her for all the right reasons. He loves her and would give his life for hers.' Julia told me she was not in any pain and was 'being called home.' She was happy and had a great life, wonderful family and amazing journey."

Ruth was sobbing, "Thank you, Annie."

They both continued to sit in silence, lost in their thoughts.

Annie was thinking that she had left out a crucial piece that Julia had told her, but she believed it wasn't her truth to tell Ruth. In the dream, Julia had continued, "Annie, when Ruthie has her crisis of faith, her dark night of the soul (and you know exactly what that looks like - you have been there), please promise you will be there for her. That you will never turn your back on her regardless of what she does or says."

Annie replied, "Julia, never ever worry about Ruth. I owe her and you my life. I will always be there for her no matter where she is or what she does, I swear." Annie continued pondering the dream while watching the clouds pass by the window and sipped her wine.

Suddenly, Annie jumped out of her seat, "Holy shit, holy shit. No way!"

"What, what?"

"Hey, not to make this moment all about me...I remember where I heard about the Blue Rose. Your mom!"

"My mom? Are you sure? No kidding?"

"No shit! Julia also said that night, 'Protect Ruthie; she can be too trusting.'"

"Not anymore," Ruth interjected. "I learned after mom died and all the rumors started about my family that trust is not easily given."

"Ruth!"

"Right, I'll stop interrupting. I'm listening."

Annie continued, "She said, 'Annie, you'll be fine. Your answers are at the blue rose. All will be well.' And just like that, your mother disappeared, or I woke up...I don't really know what happened. I looked at my watch, it was 11:11 and I texted you."

Ruth and Annie both started to cry harder.

Annie looked at Ruth, "Do you think your mom told Mike to hold back the damn financing? Is this all her doing?" Ruth started to answer and realized it was a joke.

"I should have told you sooner, Ruth, but you never asked, so I thought she came to you as well."

"No, you were always her favorite daughter," Ruth said, winking.

"That's true, but I didn't inherit the fucking island, did I?"

"Ladies," Jake announced, "we shall be landing at the Blue Rose airport, if you can call it an airport, in twenty-five minutes. Please prepare for landing."

They landed at 3:30 p.m. and there was not another plane in sight.

Ruth stood up, looking at Annie. "OK, Annie, chop chop, get off the plane so I can start my vacation away from you!"

"You'll miss me," Annie said, grabbing her bag and laptop and heading to the door to deplane.

"Hey, Annie?"

"Yes, Ruth, dear."

"Do you?"

"Do I what?"

"Do you really want to grow the company?" Ruth asked, cautious of how to frame the question.

Annie looked at her and walked down the steps. Halfway across the tarmac she stopped, looked back at Ruth, and yelled, "I don't know. I really don't know, Ruth." She turned around and kept walking toward the rental car lot.

At the house on the beach, Annie pulled into the cobblestone driveway and, after the garage door opened automatically, drove into the large three-car garage. It took a few minutes to find the alarm box located behind the shelves, but after she typed in 8976, the door unlocked and the alarm deactivated.

Annie walked into the kitchen, set down her bag and stopped to enjoy the most stunning view of the ocean. Mike had made the home sound like a small little cottage located on a tiny beach, but in reality it was a three-thousand-square-foot house, on a large secluded lot in a gated community. The view was one of the most spectacular Annie had seen, and considering how much she traveled that was saying a lot.

"*This is amazing,*" Annie said to no one, as she walked over and opened the refrigerator. It was fully stocked. "*Who does that?*" Next stop the wine refrigerator. She was sure it would be jammed packed with the finest wines, and flung the door open with great anticipation. Inside was water and diet coke. "*Come on Mike, really? Not a drop of wine? Who seriously does that?*" Annie was thinking as she quickly unloaded her tablet. She typed wine stores into her search engine, but came up with nothing. Liquor store? Nothing. "Where in the hell do people buy their booze?" she yelled, exasperated.

"At the corner market," a voice from the garage called out. Annie jumped five feet in the air and whipped around. Standing in front of her was a Hispanic woman, about 4'8", slim, with long black hair, black eyes that seemed to look through her, and a Texas-sized grin. "Hi Annie, I'm Maria. I wanted to see if you need anything."

After her heart stopped pounding through her chest, Annie managed a weak, "Wine. Mike has none."

"The Blue Rose market has great wines and delivers. Want me to order for you?" Maria asked.

"No, just give me the number and I'll take care of it," Annie responded.

"I'll text you the number. If you don't need anything else, then I'll be off."

Annie thought for a moment. "Maria, I'm fine...I'll only be here until Monday so I don't need much at all."

"That's what you think," Maria yelled over her shoulder on her way out the door.

"Wait, what did you say?" Annie yelled towards the door. "Come back here, what did you say?" *"She's as nutty as Mike if she thinks I'm staying here past Monday. The plane will be wheels-up by 5:00pm! Anyway, onto more important things, such as ordering wine. I am sure there will be a long wait."*

"Blue Rose Market, this is Kevin, how may I serve you?"

"Hello Kevin, this is Annie Walker over at Mike Williams' place. I would like to order some wine."

"Yes, Miss Walker, what can I get you?"

"I would like six bottles of your best red, a bottle of your best vodka, and please can you have it delivered?"

"Yes ma'am, I'll be on my way shortly."

"How long?"

"Five minutes."

"Are you serious? No one moves that fast!"

"We do," Kevin answered. "Anything else?"

"Do you have a cheese and fruit plate?"

"Not here, but the coffee shop has a great one. I'll stop by, pick one up and be on my way. That means I will arrive in about ten minutes. Is that satisfactory for you?"

"Ahhh, yes it is. Thanks, Kevin."

"See you soon, Mrs. Walker."

Ten minutes later there was a knock on the door, and a tall lanky kid, about sixteen, well-tanned with surfer blonde hair, was standing there. Annie opened the door, Kevin walked in with the wine and a cheese platter on top of that. He placed the wine in the wine fridge and cheese platter in the refrigerator. "Is there anything else I can get for you?"

"Not right now." Annie was so shocked at the level of customer service all she could think of was whether she could hire Kevin away. "I'm fine. How much do I owe you?"

"Mr. Williams took care of it, and also asked that I give you this note," he said, handing a blue envelope to Annie.

"Well, here is a tip." Annie handed him a $100 bill.

"Can't accept that. Mr. Williams took care of the tip as well."

"Kevin, I am guessing you are in high school and working at your folks' store. You surf when you can but you are balancing school, work and surfing, correct?"

"Yes, ma'am."

"Kevin, never turn money down. Maybe when you are a millionaire, but until then, take it, bank it and move on. OK?" A big smile came over Kevin's face as he took the $100 bill and gently placed it into his wallet.

"Thanks. This will go right into my new-car fund. I'll check back Monday to see if you need anything else."

"Don't bother - I am leaving Monday."

As Kevin was walking out the back door he yelled, "See you Monday."

"This town is crazy. They must be lonely and hoping for new folks to talk to. I'll be on that plane," Annie thought as she opened a bottle of wine; glancing over at the clock, she saw it read 5:15 p.m. She carried the cheese platter over to the patio where all the furniture was facing the ocean and the BBQ area was over on the side.

"Wow, it's been a long time since I've been just sitting around at 6:45 with nowhere to go. No investor meetings, nothing family related, just sitting and being bored. I even forgot to bring a book." Annie walked outside to a lounge chair perfectly position in the surf. Watching the waves come in and go back out, sipping wine, she was thinking how amazing it tasted and pondering if she should really be sitting there doing nothing. *"I could be checking emails, looking at financials, planning whom to approach for financing."* Annie drifted off....

"Only losers sit around and do nothing. That is why, Annie, you'll never amount to much," Annie's father said, standing in the kitchen. *"You always sit around reading. Be like your brother who's a hard worker, always lending a hand around the store. Not like you,*

always studying and dreaming. Do something with your life."

"Dad, I have a test tomorrow that I have to pass."

"Why? You'll never make it to college, and even if you did, we can't pay. We promised to pay for your brother," her father said, walking away and shaking his head.

"Adopted brother," Annie mumbled.

Suddenly, Annie jerked awake and saw it was totally dark; her watch said it was 1:30 a.m. She stumbled as she stood, trying to get from the chair to the house, where she finally lay down and passed out.

Chapter 4

"Frick, the sun shines bright here! What time is it?" Annie had forgotten to close the curtains and the sun was streaming through the large glass window in the master bedroom. *"Damn it, why didn't I pull the curtain?"* Annie thought, as she tried to focus her eyes. *"All this fresh air does is give this city girl a headache. May as well get up and grab an aspirin."* On the kitchen counter the empty bottle of wine was sitting next to the opened vodka bottle. Annie stared at them and wondered, *"When will this end? When will I get it together and forget? Just fucking forget! Just have peace. Will I ever know what peace is?"*

Shaking her head, she noticed the blue envelope from Mike that Kevin had left, sitting unopened on the counter.

Annie opened the letter. "Hi Annie. I am so glad you accept my offer." *"Like I had a choice,"* Annie thought. "If you need anything at all, Maria and Kevin are ready to help. Take time, Annie, to relax and take a walk on the beach. The ocean air will help clear your thoughts. Please do me a favor and stop by the Blue Rose Bookstore and say hello to my old friend Bredra. Who knows, you may find something magical there. Annie, I have been EXACTLY where you are right now. I understand what you are going through better than you think. Watch your drinking. Good luck and here is to you Finding Your Blue Rose. Love, Mike."

"WTF does that mean? Watch my drinking? Hell, everyone knows Mike was a raging drunk back in the day. I'm far from that. Sure, a few drinks here and there

but not an out of control drunk. His wife left him, and that's why he got it together. Something magical may happen? That's what Kevin said last night. This town makes people cuckoo-cachoo. I've been exactly where you are? Seriously Mike you have no idea!"

"Mom, why does dad hate me?"

"Honey, he doesn't hate you, he just doesn't understand girls."

"So that's why he likes the adopted son better."

"Don't say that, Annie - you are both our children."

Still sitting in the kitchen, Annie was sure it had to be around 10:00 and that meant it was breakfast wine time. *"That will help keep me hydrated while I go through the financials."* Annie poured a glass of wine, carried it out to the patio, and opened the financials.

Walking back into the kitchen, Annie glanced at the clock and was surprised to see it was already 3:30 in the afternoon. She started to laugh, *"That's what happens when I look at financials. I completely lose track of time. But now I know what buildings we can pull money out of to invest in new builds. These beach days seem to fly by."* Opening her laptop, she saw there were over five hundred emails and most were marked urgent. *"I'm sure only about thirty are actually urgent."* Sipping her wine, she started reading and forwarding the emails. *"I love being the boss!"*

Noticing her wine glass was empty again, she decided it would be much easier to take the bottle outside with her. Grabbing the bottle she wondered why everyone was so concerned about her drinking. *"I've got everything under control,"* Annie thought, as she poured another glass of wine....

"What are you doing?"
"Studying."
"Why? Mom and Dad will never pay for you to go to college, only me," he said, cooking dinner.
"We'll see. I will go to college one way or another."
"No, dumb ass, you're too stupid."
"It might be you're the dumb ass."

He walked over slowly, leaned over, pressed a red-hot fork on her back and held it there.

She screamed at the top of her lungs in pain. It was the most excruciating pain she had ever felt. All she could do was cry.

"Never talk to me like that again. Clean up the kitchen and go to bed, you pathetic piece of shit."

Annie remembered the cheese plate she had left on the kitchen counter. Standing up, she tripped over the empty wine bottles and face-planted on the patio. Her knee ripped open on a wooden plank and blood started flowing like a stream. Doing her best to stand, she dragged herself to the kitchen for a towel. There was blood everywhere; Annie was trying her best to stop the bleeding with one hand and clean up the mess with the other.

"Miss Annie, Miss Annie, are you all right?" Maria screamed as she flung open the backdoor. "I'll call the ambulance right away. This is terrible, horrible…I'll call the ambulance."

"No, don't please!" Annie whispered as she tried to wave Maria off. "Just help me to the bathroom. I'm fine. I just need a bandage." Annie knew the last thing she needed was someone to call Nick or Ruth and tell them about this. They would instantly guess she had been drinking and wouldn't listen to what really happened. "Maria, I just tripped over the floor board heading on the patio."

Before Annie had arrived, Mike had spoken to Maria about Annie and had asked Maria to keep an eye on her. "Maria, trust me…on the outside she is totally put together, but inside there is something that just simmers. She has problems and she is not yet ready to face them. Remember how you found me many years ago when we first met?"

"Yes, Mr. Mike, I will never forget."

"That's where she is now. We just need to gently but firmly guide her to find her way."

"I'll watch her closely and ask Kevin to as well."

"Maria, you see, Annie claims to be clumsy, and I used to tell people the exact same thing. She's a very proud woman and the best friend a person could ever have. There was a lady who worked for Annie back in the early days of her company whose son was killed in an accident. Annie hired a private plane to fly the woman home, paid for the funeral and paid her salary for two months. Heart of gold is what everyone sees, but I see the inner turmoil. Maria, call me if she runs into real trouble, otherwise just try to keep her safe during these next few days."

So when Mike received a text from Kevin that Annie had ordered "a lot of wine," he immediately called Maria and left a message asking her to run over and check on her. When she saw the message a few hours later, she drove over, to find Annie bleeding on the floor. She found steri-strips to bandage up the knee the best she could.

"Maria, please get me a glass of vodka for the pain."

Maria hesitated.

Annie could sense her hesitation, "Never mind, Maria. Can you please be discreet and keep this quiet? Maybe not mention this to Mike? I'll pay to clean up."

"No need, Miss Annie; I have a cleaning crew on speed dial."

Annie stood there trying to comprehend that statement. *Who has a cleaning crew on call?* All Annie could say out loud was, "Fascinating."

Maria changed the subject. "Miss Annie, when you get tired of eating cheese, please try Terri's Tea and Coffee Shop in town. They have the best food and all kinds of exotic teas, plus it's right across from the Blue Rose Bookstore. Have you gone to the Blue Rose Bookstore yet?"

Before Annie could turn around and ask why everyone obsession with that bookstore, Maria was gone.

Chapter 5

"Ruth, are you busy? Got a second?" Annie whispered into the phone.

"Annie? What's wrong?" Ruth asked, in a puzzled, worried tone. Annie had always been strong regardless of what was going on around her. In the more than thirty years she had known Annie she had never heard her sound so weak, so tired, so defeated.

When Annie and Ruth first met in their college dorm room, Annie acted like she owned the room. Over the years that followed, they had been through some really bad times and Annie was always the strong one people flocked to for reassurance.

"Ruth?" There was a pause that seemed to last forever. "Ruth, can I ask you a question? I need the truth." Annie hesitated, trying to decide if she wanted to ask the question or just hang up. "Ruth, do you think I drink too much?"

Ruth slowly took a long deep breath then quietly answered, "Yes."

The line went dead.

Ruth stood in the hotel lobby trying to decide if she should call Annie back or fly in and check on her. But Ruth remembered the conversation she had with Mike before the last board meeting, when he made her promise to leave Annie alone. "Ruth, you have to let Annie figure things out for herself. You, more than anyone else, know she has her inner battles."

"Agreed, Mike, I'll leave her alone, unless she calls and asks for help. I will never say no to her. Her whole childhood she was left on her own. I promised myself in our freshman year I would never do that to her. Deal?"

Mike was genuinely shocked to hear that Ruth agreed with his assessment of Annie. Mike finally answered, "That is so sad. Why do you think she's so lost, so in pain? She seems to have everything a person could ask for. Ruth, I've never asked, but you're her best friend and of all people you have to know why."

"Mike, it's her story, her truth, and not for me to say. We each have our truth and it is for each of us to understand and share that truth when we are ready."

"Understood," Mike nodded in agreement.

Now, after Maria left, Annie hobbled out to the beach and stared at the vastness of the ocean and this universe. *"The wonder of it all...."* she thought as a school of dolphins went by. Seashells were rolling up with the waves then back out. For Annie, the waves came in at a soothing pace.

The next morning, Annie woke up starving. She decided it was time to venture out to the town. She showered, put on a pair of pink Capri shorts, a knit white scoop neck sweater, sandals and a matching wide brim hat. Looking in the mirror, Annie thought *"I look damn good for a woman my age."* Laughing to herself, she walked outside and heard her stomach growl so loudly she was sure the neighbors could hear it.

Walking down the driveway, Annie was overwhelmed with all the flowers surrounding the house. It was like a floral explosion of wonderful scents and colors that was visually stunning. *"I wonder when I last stopped and even notice my surroundings? Maybe when we were in Paris?"* Annie thought, looking for a sign directing her to the city. When she didn't see a sign, she decided that since she was left-handed, left was the way to go. The song "Follow the Yellow Brick Road" started playing in her head.

Suddenly the town seemed to appear out of nowhere. There were a few storefronts and each was a cornucopia of color; it looked like "Whoville." Each storefront - Ike's Ice Cream, Gina's Grocery, Henry's Haberdasher, Fred's Fine Dining, Jake's Jewelry, and Angie's Apparel - faced the ocean.

Oddly, Annie noticed only two stores that were located directly on the beach, Brodie's Beach Rental and The Blue Rose Bookstore.

"There it is, that damn bookstore everyone talks about," Annie thought, looking over at the store. The entrance was plain, underwhelming to say the least, a white building with a blue door. *"If this is where mystical things happen, this town is in trouble."* Annie thought, laughing to herself as she walked over to Terri's Tea & Coffee shop.

She walked up the four stairs to the shop, passed a few small white tables, pulled open the screen door and walked in. There were five tables lining the window side that offered a great beach view. On the other side were cases filled with donuts, rolls, brownies, cookies and an assortment of deli sandwiches. The aromas were making Annie's mouth water and reminding her how hungry she was.

A young man about seventeen years old walked over, wearing a crisp, white apron that had "Terri's Tea & Coffee" printed across the front in blue. "How may I help you, ma'am?" Annie looked at her wrist to check the time and realized she wasn't wearing her watch.

'What time is it?" Annie asked the young man.

"Mrs. Walker, it's about 11:00."

"Really, that late?"

'Yes ma'am. How can I serve you today?"

"How about an iced tea and...gosh, I'm hungry. What do you recommend, Tim?" Annie asked, glancing at his name tag.

"Our Italian sandwich is very popular. In fact it's my favorite."

"Great. Then I'll have an iced tea, Italian sandwich on wheat, and what the hell, French fries."

"OK, Mrs. Walker, have a seat and I'll bring it to you. May I suggest you sit outside on this beautiful sunny day at the ocean?"

"Great idea, Tim. Hey, what the heck, add a chocolate chip cookie."

She walked outside, selected the chair closest to the ocean and watched people walk by. A few people were swimming and there were several surfers in the distance. *"This is a spectacular view...no wonder Mike loves it here. Wonder how much a house like his would cost to own? Maybe Nick and I could look into living here in a few years, after we grow the company. But who has time to sit around when there is so much work to be done?"* Annie quickly dismissed that thought.

"Here you go - enjoy!" Tim said as he set down the beautiful crystal plate with a large sandwich overflowing with pepperoni, salami, and cheese on fresh, warm wheat bread. "I forgot to ask if you wanted it toasted so I did. If you would prefer it untoasted I'll take it back."

"No way, it's perfect...thanks."

"Just let me know if you would like anything else, Mrs. Walker."

"Will do," Annie said taking her first bite. *"This is a great... I was so hungry."* She devoured that sandwich in no time. Remembering she had ordered a cookie she started to look for it, and just then Tim reappeared and set down the largest cookie Annie had ever seen. It was warm, gooey and smelled like heaven. Tim also served her a glass of ice cold milk.

"Service is amazing here. If I lived here this would be my favorite place." Annie took a little bit more time eating the cookie than she did the sandwich. She couldn't quit staring at the bookstore across the street; it was as if the store was calling her. It looked very different from all the other buildings, but Annie couldn't figure out why other than that it was located directly on the beach.

In high school Annie had dreamt of owning a bookstore. She told her mother it had to be on the beach and a band would play each night. There would be a bar so people could have beverages as they perused the books. It would be packed with people wanting to read and make new friends. They could sell their books or just share with others. Her mother was never a reader and thought it was the stupidest idea Annie ever had. But then according to her mother, most of her ideas were dumb.

"You will never make money. Just concentrate on finding a man. Even you should be able to do that," her mother would say.

Walking away, Annie whispered back, "Leaders are readers, Mother! If I plan to take over the family business I need to be able to read financials and to do that I have to go to college."

"You never know what the future holds, Annie, but I am sure it is not a used bookstore with a bar. For the love of God, how do you even think of these things?"

"No idea, I just do, Mom."

This was the first time in ages Annie had remembered that conversation with her mother. Her mother had always underestimated her in everything she did while her adopted brother, Bobbie, was king of the house. They wanted so badly for him to take over the business although he was dumber than a box of rocks. They saw something in him that no one else on the planet saw. *"Blind parental love,"* Annie thought.

"Hey Tim, have you ever visited the bookstore across the street?" Annie asked the waiter while he was bussing the tables.

"Of course – it's magical."

"I'm thinking of walking over to get a book."

"Hey I hate to ask a favor, Mrs. Walker, but Bredra, the bookstore owner, always orders a sandwich with fresh brewed iced tea around noon and there's no one here but me. Would you mind taking it over to her?"

Blue Rose Bookstore: the Gift of Why

"Not at all. Let me pay up and I'll take it over."

"There's no check. Mr. Mike never allows his guests to pay."

"Come on, Tim, give me the check."

"If I did, I would get in so much trouble with my parents and Mr. Mike. Please don't ask!"

"Annie, Tim...please call me Annie."

"You bet, Mrs. Walker," Tim said, walking away.

Annie got up, grabbed the white bag marked Terri's Tea and Coffee, threw a $100.00 bill on the table, and walked across the narrow cobblestone street to the bookstore.

Part II The Bookstore

Chapter 6

Crossing the street, Annie balanced the food and drink in one hand, opened the wooden door to the bookstore with the other, and as she did a bell rang out. The musty smell of books permeated the air. There were books on shelves, books on the floor, books piled in every corner, books out the back door towards the beach. "This must be what heaven looks like!" Annie said out loud, like a little girl in her favorite candy store.

Annie saw a woman standing in the store - in her mid-80s, tall and thin, with grey spikey hair, wearing baggy white cuffed shorts, a yellow striped blouse and flip flops. "Hi Annie! I wondered when you would stop by."

"You must be Bredra...Tim asked me to deliver this to you," Annie said walking towards the woman to hand her the bag.

"Thank you. I do love their sandwiches. Want a bite?"

Chuckling, Annie declined, "I have to get going." Her knee was starting to hurt and she decided against looking for a book. Annie thought that propping her leg up at Mike's and having a drink sounded wonderful. She slowly walked back towards the bookstore entrance, then turned around and asked, "How do you know my name? I didn't tell you."

"This is a small town, Annie. Mike told me about you a few years ago."

"Really? A couple of years ago? Seriously? What was that conversation all about?" Annie was curious as to why Mike would talk about her with a stranger who owned a bookstore in some obscure city.

Bredra sat down in a wrought iron chair next to the bar, "Can I interest you in an iced tea?"

"No thanks, I can't stay."

"Oh? Busy day planned?"

"I have work to do."

"What work do you do?"

"I work in senior housing."

"Doing?"

"Doing senior housing."

Bredra laughed. "Annie, it's just a question. I don't want anything from you, just making conversation."

It was Annie's turn to laugh, "You are right, I'm just being an ass. I own a few senior housing communities across the coast. Well really, I own fifteen and am getting ready to buy more, many more."

"Is that what you want?"

"Huh...what? Of course. In fact, Mike is on my Advisory Board and is helping me secure the funding for the purchase."

"Mike's a great guy. Did he tell you I helped him a few years back?"

"Really? No, what did you do for him?"

"He had some challenges."

"Oh yeah, with the drinking? He told me about those days."

"You could say that," Bredra answered with a twinkle in her eye. "Annie, do you have children?"

"A boy and girl. Nickolas and Emma."

"They both work for the family business, I assume."

"You betcha. Nickolas is preparing to take over the company, at least in his mind," Annie said. laughing. "He is so eager for me to retire it makes me laugh. I always have to tell him to dial it back - it'll happen when it does."

"When do you think it will be? Your retirement, that is." Bredra asked curiously.

"Not for a few years. I want to grow the company to about fifty communities, sell it, and then ride off into the sunset. Nickolas doesn't agree with that vision."

"Then what will you do?"

"Geez," Annie said with fake exasperation, "you ask a shit ton of questions. Who knows? Maybe buy a house on the beach and read. Maybe own a vineyard. Of course, I don't like to sit around too long, so the beach idea might not work."

"I like to get to know my customers. You look like a reader so I plan on selling you a few books," Bredra continued, laughing. She had a deep belly laugh that sounded like Santa Claus and caused everyone around her to laugh along.

"I'm sure you will, Bredra. I love bookstores, love to read."

"Keeps your mind occupied?"

"I guess. I'll take you up on a drink," Annie replied. "Anything stronger than iced tea?"

"Help yourself, this is a self-service bookstore. You will be spending some time here so familiarize yourself with everything."

Annie poured herself a glass of wine from the bar. "Nice thought, but I don't think so. I am going back home Monday - that's when they bring the plane back."

"You have your own plane?"

"Yes, but it's not what you think. I travel a lot and it saves me a ton of time having my own plane."

"Whoa, I'm not judging, I'm just asking. Are you always this defensive?"

"No, however in my position I have to be careful."

Annie was standing behind the bar sipping her glass of wine, "This is really good wine. Is it from Argentina?"

"No idea. Kevin delivers everything I need. Ask him."

"I will. It's really good."

"So why are you really here?"

"What is your trip? Enough with all the questions. I'm here because Tim asked me to bring over your sandwich."

"You love the ocean, don't you?"

"Oh my God, yes - I find it calming, filled with possibilities, innocent, soothing."

"How can an ocean be innocent?"

"I don't know. I'm not sure why I even said that. When I am at the ocean I feel a calmness that I feel nowhere else. I'm at peace, real true peace. I feel loved. Stop, please. Stop with the questions; this is nuts." Annie finished her wine and started looking around the bookstore.

Changing the subject, Annie asked, "Why is this called the Blue Rose Bookstore? I don't see any blue roses anywhere."

Bredra looked out at the ocean surf, cleared her throat and said, "Have you ever seen a blue rose? Not a dyed blue rose but one grown in an actual garden?"

"Never gave it a thought but…no."

"That's because they are impossible to grow in nature right now. There is a genetic reason that I won't bore you with; just trust me. Through the years the blue rose has come to signify accomplishing the impossible, fighting all odds and starting with a new beginning. It's also considered enchanted, magical, spiritual with a dash of mystery."

"Now that's cool. Great name, very well selected. You could do some great marketing around that name," Annie said walking back towards the bar.

"The vodka is on the first shelf in the middle cupboard." Bredra pointed to it as she sipped her tea.

"Thanks." Annie found a water glass, filled it with vodka, opened the refrigerator, grabbed a lemon, sliced off a piece, threw it into the glass and took a gulp.

"You drink a lot."

"Are you kidding me?"

"What happened to your knee, Annie? Why the bandage?"

"None of your damn business."

"You know, you need to mellow out. Not every conversation leads to OSS."

"What is OSS?"

"Other Shoe Syndrome. When one thing goes wrong, the other shoe will always drop. You learned that in childhood, didn't you?"

"Screw you! I have no idea what the hell you are even talking about."

"Annie," Bredra continued talking, "you graduated from a top ten university, you're happily married, you have great children who adore you, you are more successful than 90% of people in this country, you've been featured in all major media outlets and have more money than you'll ever spend. So, young-un, when will enough be enough?"

Annie took a large gulp from her drink and snapped, "Where did that come from?"

"When are you going to do what you really want to do? When are you going to stop trying to prove your worth to everyone? You are good enough! Isn't it time to let yourself off the hook?"

"Excuse me. I mean, *excuse me*?"

"You have to figure out two things before you will ever move forward. The first is why you haven't secured financing to purchase the package of communities and...."

Annie quickly interrupted "Let me guess - the second is why I drink so much?"

"No, young-un. You already know the answer to that question but you have yet to accept that it wasn't your fault. The second is your Why? What is your WHY behind everything? Once you understand your Why, that will help you discover the gift contained within and you'll finally find your Blue Rose! More importantly, you will stop living in so much pain."

Annie glared at Bredra, gulped her drink, slammed the glass down, and walked towards the door. "You are a piece of work. Why don't you go find someone else to analyze? Someone with real problems who wants to answer those two questions. Not my fault? No shit. Living in pain? You have no idea. So I say, fuck you."

Bredra started laughing so hard tears were rolling down her cheek, which enraged Annie. Stopping dead in her tracks Annie spun around to face Bredra. "What do you find so damn funny?"

"So this is the famous Annie's 'don't fuck with me' attitude I've heard so much about. To be honest, I never thought I would see it so fast."

"My what?"

"Come on, Annie. You know it's your 'don't fuck with me' attitude. It's your way of intimidating people to keep them at a distance. That way they don't get close and hurt you. I'm guessing it works well, because it's your go to defense, FAST."

"Who told you about that? What else do you think you know?" Annie turned, opening the front door. "Because you know nothing about me!" Annie shouted, slamming the door behind her.

Annie thought she heard Bredra whisper, "Annie, I can help you."

She walked fast, almost running back to the house. Her knee started to bleed but she didn't care. All she could do was cry. Once she arrived home she could tell Maria had been there. The refrigerator was cleaned and restocked, leaving enough food and drink for a few more days.

"I don't know why all the damn food - I am leaving...now!" Annie picked up the vodka, filled the water glass, added an ice cube and slice of lemon, and sat on the patio.

She grabbed her cell phone and started dialing, "You have reached the voicemail of Ruth Watson. I'm unavailable to answer the phone. Please leave your name, number and message I will return your call."

"Ruth, call me! I have to get out of here. Send the plane NOW! You can stay on vacation but it's time for me to get back to work. Screw the financing - I figured out a different way to secure the money."

Her phone vibrated; it was a text from Ruth.

"Annie, can't call...spotty phone reception on the island. Nickolas told me the plane has mechanical issues and won't be ready for few more days. He doesn't know at this time when. Sorry, should have told you sooner."

"*Next week? No fucking way!*" Annie texted back, "Never mind, I'll fly commercial. See you back at the office."

"Annie, remember? Only private planes can get in and out of that airport."

"That's helpful, *not*. Get the fucking plane working."

"Sure, let me get right on that. You know what? I'll wave my magic wand and fix it. Wait, it's fixed."

"Thanks for nothing." Annie slammed her phone down on the table and took a large drink.

Ruth texted, "The water is really warm and the island is great, thanks for asking."

"You're dead to me."

Ruth decided not to respond. She knew Annie's temper all too well.

Taking another sip of her drink, Annie reflected on her conversation with Bredra. "*What did Bredra* mean, 'I know'? Know what? I'm an open book. Hell, my whole life is on the Internet. The good, the bad, all posted online for all to see. Wedding pictures, business pictures, grand openings, you name it you can find it online. How did she know some of that stuff about me? And the OSS?"

Staring at the ocean water, Annie suddenly heard Julia's voice in her mind. *"The answer is at the Blue Rose."*

"What answers? Where did that come from? Hell, I don't even understand the question. How can I find an answer? Could she have meant Bredra's stupid two questions?" Annie wondered. "I should call Ruth back and tell her I'm sorry."

Chapter 7

"Come on, Annie, let's go back to the dorm."

"Come on, Ruth, just one more drink?"

Ruth and Annie were at the Bar in the Woods, aptly named because it was actually a bar in the woods. Everyone from the college went there at least once or twice a month to listen to the live band and dance.

"You have had enough. Let's go."

"You go, Ruth. I'll catch a ride or drive home."

"You...drive?"

"Sure! I just played Mario Carts, didn't crash once so I am good to go."

"You're kidding, aren't you?"

"No, that really is how we decide who drives when you're not here. Come on, Ruth, you have to get out more."

"I get out enough, and if I got a DWI my father would kill me."

"Ah yeah. The Governor would be a bit miffed. Could be a career ender, at least to your political career," Annie said, laughing.

"I'm not interested in running for office. I want to be a chief of staff and a DWI would end that dream. My 4.0 would be wasted."

"Oh my God, not the grades again! You are all about the grades."

Annie was slurring her words, wobbling towards the car. "You'll be surprised when you learn grades and where you graduate from don't matter."

"What's important to you then, smarty-pants?"

"Innovation. Seeing the future before the next guy. Relationship building, hell, building the future!"

"We'll see who is right in a few years when we graduate. Until then, get in the car, my friend."

As Annie was opening the passenger side door, their friend Mooky was getting out of his car. "Hey, where are you going?" He grabbed Annie around the waist. "Let's go get a drink."

"Sure, let's go."

"No!" Ruth yelled to Annie. "Get in the car!"

Mooky turned to Annie. "If you must go, how about a kiss?"

"Sure, for a beer," Annie said playfully.

He walked over and planted a long kiss on her and asked again, "Are you sure you don't want to stay?"

"I'll stay."

"No, she won't and shame on you, Mooky. You're engaged, you dumb ass, and your girlfriend is inside. Annie, what about Nick?"

"Ruth, you are a buzz kill," Mooky answered, "but you make an excellent point. Here's the beer I promised you." Mooky handed it to Annie and headed to the front door.

Annie suddenly spun around and stared at Ruth. "Don't you worry, ever, about me and Nick. I'm not married to him. It is what it is. I'll do what I damn well please. Got it?"

"Annie, you know you'll do anything for a drink."

"Shut up, Ruth." Annie got into the car and slammed the door. "Don't worry about me drinking, taking drugs or anything else. It's none of your damn business what I do. You're not my mother. And if you keep this up you won't be my friend either."

"Annie, you know you can't intimidate me with that bullshit attitude. I know everyone else backs down, but I never will. Trust me!"

"Fuck you. Just back the fuck off."

"Sure, dear. That, my friend, is why we are friends! You need someone who likes you for you and ask nothing in return."

They drove in silence as Ruth navigated the narrow, poorly-lit back roads, hilly, with twists and turns that people liked to drive fast on. It was like a roller coaster ride. No one quite understood why someone put a bar in a wooded area five miles from a town. Of course, the bar was extremely popular. Because it was far away, noise was never an issue so the band could play as loud as they wanted.

They had been driving for a while and Ruth thought Annie had passed out.

"I'm sorry," Annie said quietly.

"No apology is ever needed."

"But sometimes it's necessary," Annie continued. "Thanks for being my friend. I know it can be hard, really hard."

"Annie, I love you like a sister; you never need to worry about our friendship."

"Have you figured it out, Ruth? Do you know?"

Know what? Ruth didn't know how to answer. Her mind was racing trying to figure out what Annie was referring to. They had many deep conversations since meeting telling each other everything. They talked about families, dreams, hopes, goals, whether to get married and have children. Ruth even told Annie she was unable to have children due to an accident years before. They talked about anything and everything. She always sensed Annie was holding something back, but she never asked. Her instincts told her that was an area where she never wanted to go.

"Did you know I had my first drink when I was about four?" Annie whispered.

"Ummmm," was all Ruth could say out loud. Inside, she was screaming, "What??? Are you kidding me? Were you raised in a bar? Were your parents wolves? They seemed so nice when I met them."

"When it first happened, he gave me a beer and made me drink it, fast. Then he forced me take off all my clothes." Her voice trailed off, lost in thought. It was as if she was reliving the experience.

"Hmmmmm...."

"The first memory is of him slapping me. Then it escalated to a belt and then,..." Her voice was eerily void of any emotion. It was like she was telling Ruth about a movie she had just seen. But she was talking about her life!

Ruth thought, "And she was just a kid? This is the most surreal experience I think I have even had."

"As time went on it became more aggressive, more physical. You know what I mean, right?"

Ruth realized she was holding her breath, and wanted to scream, "No, I have no idea what you mean! This is something you see in a movie, not something you hear driving home from a bar. Oh my dear God, what do I say?"

Annie continued, "The beatings really weren't that bad; it was the sex," Annie said as she took a deep, long, sad sigh. Annie's voice had a level of sadness, hurt, that Ruth had never heard from anyone before, ever. Not even when her beloved grandmother passed away unexpectedly and her father was devastated. Who was Annie talking about? Her father always seemed so nice but I guess you never know.

"My adopted brother was one sick bastard."

"You had a brother"? Ruth panicked. They were best friends but Annie never, ever, mentioned a brother!

Annie didn't answer. She crossed her arms over her chest, almost as if she was trying to hold herself, and stared out the window. Driving into town past a street lamp, Ruth saw tears pouring down Annie's face. They drove in silence the rest of the way home.

The girls never spoke again about that night or Annie's childhood. Ruth was never really sure if Annie even remembered the conversation.

Chapter 8

Annie was jolted awake by her cell phone. Half asleep, still drunk from the night before, she answered, "Hello, Annie Walker."

"Hi Mom," Nickolas said quickly. "Hey, got a minute? I want to tell you about the plane. It's my fault. I should have called you after I found out. But the old girl will be ready Tuesday, maybe, I hope...well, who really knows? But when it's ready, Mom, I'll send it to pick up Ruth then you. Sound like a plan, Mom? Mom, are you there?"

"Yes...what time is it, Nickolas?" Annie asked.

"Oh crap, Mom, I just realized its only 5:00 a.m. where you are. Crap, sorry Mom."

"Nickolas, don't worry about it. I fell asleep early last night reading financials," Annie fibbed. "Before you send the plane, please call me first and let me know, OK?"

"Sure Mom, but Ruth said you were ready to come back. In fact, she said you were pissed the plane was down."

"No, not anymore, I understand. Please Nickolas, can you just do as I ask?"

"Sure, Mom. Hey, Dad says hi. Emma says hi and Rosie the bulldog says hi and we all miss you."

"I love you and miss you guys too, Nickolas."

"Love you too, mom...'bye." Hanging up he paused...*did she sound strange?* He started to redial then changed his mind, and instead texted Ruth. "Do you think Mom is OK?" Because Ruth was unable to have children, Annie and Nick had asked her to be godmother to both their children. Since they were born Ruth had showered them with love and gifts.

'Yes, Nick, she's fine. Just give her space...she needs to think. To work things out."

"All Mom does is think." Nick texted back.

"True, Nickolas, but she needs to make decisions."

"Hopefully about retiring so I can become the CEO and grow this company to one- to two-hundred communities."

"Slow down, Nickolas. Your time is coming. Relax. Learn. Never forget your mother is an amazing business woman who got this company where it is."

"I know. She started with nothing and built all this. Ruth, I admire Mom and everything she has accomplished. But I get the feeling, well, really Emma thinks this isn't Mom's passion any longer."

"Only time will tell, Nicolas. When she knows, you'll know. OK?"

"Thanks, Ruth. We are so glad to have you as a part of this family. You speak 'Mom' like none of us can, including Dad."

"Love you too, Nickolas."

After hanging up the phone, Annie slowly crawled out of bed with an alcohol-fueled raging headache. *"You'd think I would learn."* Walking into the kitchen, she made a cup of tea and grabbed the vodka bottle to put a dash into her tea. Picking up her phone and tea, she walked outside.

Sitting in the lounge chair, she thought back to the bookstore conversation. *"What did Bredra mean by 'I* can help you?' What did Ruth mean? I'm fine. Why can't people see I am just fine?"

As she sipped her tea Annie thought, "Hell, if I am stuck here longer than a few days I might as well go get a book to read." Annie was a voracious reader and typically read three or four books each week. "Leaders are readers," she would always say. "I'll never understand why I didn't bring a book with me. Oh yeah, because of the damn enchanted bookstore. I still don't understand why all those damn questions."

Annie thought more about meeting Bredra. "Of course, there really wasn't a good reason for me to storm out like I did, but I hate when people try to pry. People always seem so interested in my damn life. If I want someone to know, I'll tell them." Sipping her tea, she realized she had forgotten the vodka. She chuckled to herself, "It must be a sign from that crazy lady at the bookstore...where magical things happen, my ass. Irritating things, but none too magical. Let's see, it's 9:00, the store opens at 10:00; that gives me time to stop and pick up a muffin as a peace offering."

Flinging the coffee shop door open, Annie yelled, "Hi, Tim, can I grab Brenda's muffin and tea? I'll take one as well." The coffee shop was packed and it seemed that once again only Tim was there working.

"That would be so darn nice of you, Miss. Annie. I am slammed again." Tim handed her the bag and cup holder. "Thanks."

"Hey Tim, can I give you some advice?"

"Sure!"

"I run a business and have two children who are itching to take over. You know why I haven't let them yet?"

"No. Why?"

"They never asked. Tell your parents you're ready to take it over. Then go and get yourself some help so you can focus on what you're really good at: customer service and innovation. Believe me, I have made millions on innovation. It will always win the day."

"I would love to start a catering and delivery service, but my parents are happy with status quo."

"Tim, they made their money. They are happy with their life and are waiting for you. Trust me on this!" Annie picked up the cup holder and bag and opening the door she yelled over her shoulder, "Tim, if you need financing, call me. My card is on the counter with my number. Good luck."

Walking across the street, Annie thought, *"I could get into being an angel investor to guys like him. Why don't I do that? Hell, why don't I do that? Maybe when I'm done growing my company, that's exactly what I'll do."*

She reached for the door of the bookshop, balancing the bag and drinks, and once again it magically opened.

"How's Tim? He's a great kid," Bredra said as Annie walked into the store.

"I helped him with a few issues and now he is ready to take over the business," Annie laughed, "at the ripe age of seventeen!"

"I gave him some advice as well. Of course you also offered to finance him, correct?"

"How did you know that?" Annie asked in a shocked voice. "There is no way he could have called you!"

"Nope, I just know you. You have a kind, sweet heart, you're whip smart, very charismatic, a gifted woman with immense talents...of course when you are willing to show that side." Bredra said in a soft voice.

"Yea, I'm just misunderstood, that's me." Annie said sarcastically. "Hey Bre, I just want to apologize for yesterday. I was rude and out of line. Actually ruder than normal."

Laughing, Bredra waved her off. "Eat your muffin while it's still warm."

When there was silence, Annie seemed to always get lost in her thoughts. It was her way of escaping, going within. Everyone had always called her a dreamer...a dreamer of impossible things...but it was a habit. She didn't quite understand it herself, but it brought her some peace while giving her a way to control her inner thoughts.

Bredra looked over at her. "Annie, young-un, dreamers turn into innovative doers."

Then clearing her throat, she asked, "Annie, when you were younger you dreamt of being a New York Times bestselling author, didn't you?"

"I did! How did you know that?"

"Why didn't or why don't you still write?"

"Hmmmm...Good question. I loved writing and thought about writing as a career. But my mom made fun of me, always calling me a dreamer. Telling me how crazy I was to think about writing a book. She would tell me you can't make any money dreaming. So, I finally decided it wasn't the path for me."

"Why did you choose business?"

"Don't really know. I guess with my parents owning a grocery store, business chose me. I knew I wanted money. I hated being poor. Not having much, I swore as a child that when I grew up I would never live like that. Seeing all Ruth and Nick had, I knew I had to have that life, too.

"Then I met Julia. She taught me so much about life - heck, more than my own mother ever did. She taught me how to carry myself, how to come across as polished and professional, how to dress, how to act depending on the environment, hell, how to eat at nice restaurants. But, to me, most important was how to decide who to trust and how people think and act. I loved her like a mother; I loved her better than my mother!"

"Annie, did the money make you feel better?"

"Well, I've been poor and I've been rich. Trust me, I like rich better. But to be honest, I thought if I had the best, top-of-the-line of everything, it would make me feel better. Help me feel whole. It didn't. It never stopped the feeling of shame. Never stopped the memories. The voices. But you already knew that, didn't you, Bredra?"

Bredra paused, giving Annie a second to collect her thoughts. "You believe you have to be more successful than anyone else and that will validate you to yourself. That will bring you happiness. Annie, when you're alone, what do you really dream about?"

"I don't dream, Bredra. I'm a pragmatist. I either do or don't do. There is no middle ground for me."

"Everyone dreams, including you. So what say

you?"

"Peace." Annie drew in a deep breath. "I guess, writing a book, traveling the world, owning a bookstore. Maybe I'll buy this one."

"That will work. My daughter owns it, so you'll have to make her an offer. I'll let her know you are interested."

"I'll have to wait twenty years - I'm not ready to sell the business yet. I still want to grow it."

"No, you don't."

"What! What do you mean? It has always been my dream to grow the company to about fifty communities, then sell."

"OK, if you truly wanted to grow it, why haven't you? You've already had three offers to sell you properties. What are you waiting for? Your son is ready and your daughter is ready. What would they say if they knew you turned down financing not once, but three times? Annie, maybe it's time to admit that chasing this dream isn't working for you because it no longer fits you. Isn't it time for you to start living in your passion? Isn't it time for you to be *you*?"

Annie remembered the last time that exact question was asked. "Isn't it time for you to be you?"

Chapter 9

Two weeks into her senior year of high school, Annie got a notice from Mrs. Day requesting her presence at the guidance office. Mrs. Day was Annie's teacher, guidance counselor, debate coach, and truly the only person who ever encouraged her.

When Annie had wanted to try out for the debate club, the previous debate teacher had told her no and reminded Annie that as a child she had a speech impediment and couldn't properly pronounce "r" or "s." Annie had worked with a speech therapist until she was a freshman in high school, when Annie flatly refused to go, and that was that.

"I'm here to see Mrs. Day."

"She is expecting you, Annie, go on in."

"Hi Annie, how are you?" Mrs. Day was probably around forty-five, with wavy black hair with a touch of grey and a petite build, and was always impeccably dressed. She was wearing a red button-down dress, a gold necklace with navy jewels in it and matching earrings.

"What's up? What did I do this time?" Annie was used to being called to the counselor's and the principal's offices.

"Annie, don't think like that. You are a smart girl filled with potential." Mrs. Day had taken over the debate team and asked Annie to join. "You are a great debater - in fact, you're the best debater on the team, quick on your feet...but for some reason your grades don't reflect this."

"I know, I know," Annie said with her head hanging down. "I try, it's just hard to concentrate at the store.

"Annie, you always seem preoccupied. Your mind wanders."

"Yes, my parents tell me that all the time. Mrs. Day, we both know I'm not very smart."

"You are! Never say that about yourself. What are you doing about college?"

"College? You know I want to go, but my parents won't pay. They want, well, almost demand I work at the store. I have applied to some colleges but no acceptance letter, yet. But I have faith. You see, my plan is to continue saving money and go to the community college first."

"How much do you have saved, if you don't mind me asking?"

"$6500."

"Wow!" Mrs. Day was quite surprised. "That's awesome!"

"I have an account at the bank. Mr. Johnson, you know, the manager over there, helped me open it back when I was twelve. Thankfully he never told my parents, and even put his name on it until I'm eighteen, which is only a few months away. You know, Mrs. Day, I am blessed that so many people seem to help me out."

"Well, add me to your fan club. Tell you what I'm going to do, Annie. I'm sure you are familiar with Hermitage College a few towns over."

"Of course. It's the private college where the elite go."

"Yes. Mrs. Bellevidere is the dean of the college. Now this has to stay between you and me...," Mrs. Walker said with a wink.

"Sure, I guess."

"We were college roommates and are still friends."

Annie must have looked shocked.

"Yes, Annie, even teachers have best friends," she said laughing. "Anyway, I will call and ask her to consider you for admission to the school."

"Wow! But I could never afford that," Annie interrupted.

"Mrs. Belvedere offers one or two scholarships a year to deserving students who she knows have potential beyond grades but can't afford the tuition. I'll personally ask her to give you one."

"Are you kidding? Why? Why be nice to me?"

"Annie, you have unlimited possibilities. You just need someone to help ignite them. But you have to make me a promise."

"What? Anything, anything at all. Yes, I'll babysit your children, wash your car, paint your house, deliver your groceries; you name it, I will do it!"

Laughing so hard she could barely speak, Mrs. Day said, "Graduate! Maintain a C average and graduate."

"I will, I promise, "Annie said, with tears rolling down her face. "Why, why are you helping me? Why?"

Annie, you are smart, pretty and filled with potential, and I'm sure there will come a time when you will realize it. I'm but one step on your path because you're destined for greatness. You're here to serve a higher calling, a higher purpose. We all see it; you are the only who doesn't."

"Thank you."

"If Mrs. Bellevidere accepts your application, the paperwork it will be sent to your house. Annie, you'll have to tell your parents."

"I will," Annie said, thinking of what could happen then.

Mrs. Day took Annie's hand and looked her straight in the eyes, saying, "If you need any help with that I'm here, OK?"

"Yes!" Annie thought..."There will be repercussions but to go to college I can hold on a little longer."

"My next appointment's here...wipe your face and remember, this conversation never happened. You applied to the college on your own...pinky swear!" They shook pinkies, and Annie walked out of the office.

The other guidance counselor walked over past Annie to Mrs. Day. "She's one odd duck."

"Trust me, there is a ton of potential buried under the attitude."

"No way, she will be in jail or skid row by the time she's twenty-one."

"Want to make a bet on that? I say in ten years she'll be a millionaire. That girl has determination, discipline, and a group of guardians watching over her. And she has that look."

"You and that look."

"Am I not always right?"

"Sure, but not this time...she has a dark side like no one else I've seen. Look at her parents...hell, they don't even believe in her. Nope, she'll be a cashier at their store until she dies. Working for her brother who has all the potential."

"A hundred bucks says I'm right."

"Deal."

"What are you thinking about, Annie?" Bredra quietly asked.

"What, huh? Sorry, I drifted off, thinking back to Mrs. Day and how I got to college."

"Mrs. Day thought highly of you."

"She was at my graduation, sitting in my parents' seats because," Annie said laughing, "I had told my parents that as a scholarship student I wasn't given seats. That still cracks me up. The kid they sacrificed to the wolves is a millionaire and their asshole adopted son runs the broken-down grocery store. That piece of shit adopted brother even had the nerve to tell me after Mom died that I didn't get a share of the store...because I didn't earn it! What a dumb ass! Seriously dude, I am married to a lawyer, you dumb fuck, my son's a lawyer, and my father-in-law is the lawyer to the stars. I buried him so deep in paper from the lawsuit I filed that he was forced to give 50% of the store to me. I got the check, sent back a note saying, 'Who's the bitch, now? YOU ARE and I own you. Fuck you.' Best money ever spent." Annie was laughing so hard she was crying.

"You also thanked Mrs. Day, didn't you?"

"Sure did. After I bought our second or third community, a classmate mentioned that Mrs. Day had cancer and they had started a car wash fundraiser. I called the hospital directly, paid all the bills and asked to remain anonymous. Two years later I decided what the hell, and paid off her mortgage. She only owed $50,000 so it wasn't a big deal."

"She knew it was you."

"How? Who told her?"

"The Universe. She was one of your 'Guardians' placed in your path to keep you moving forward."

"What? What is a Guardian?"

"There were times when you got stuck, wanted to quit, give up, even end your life, remember? But the Universe couldn't allow that. You're destiny has a higher calling, an overarching purpose, and we have to make sure you get there. So the Guardians show up when you need a push, encouragement. You share your deepest secrets with them."

"I share my secrets with no one. Not even my husband."

"Ruth?"

"What about Ruth?"

"Hey, how did you meet each other?"

"Ruth and I met my first day of college at Hermitage. We were assigned to be roommates, and if you knew Ruth you would know we are polar opposites. Especially back then. When I met her she was in a stunning red dress, black Jimmy Choo shoes, matching jewelry...and look at her mother, Julia! Julia was the First Lady, obviously married to Ruth's dad, the sitting Governor. Julia was the most stunning, classiest woman I had ever met. All three of them were all perfectly coiffed. I had never seen anything like that. They were the picture perfect family you see in commercials.

"Conversely, my parents were nothing like Ruth's family. I had two tattered suitcases that didn't match. My mom was in jeans and a shirt that said Thompson's Grocery Store. My mom, who could talk to anyone, was so uncomfortable around them...she and my dad just fidgeted. Hermitage after all, was a school of the elite, for the elite, so I truly didn't fit in. Bless Ruth...that never bothered her.

"Anyway, mom and dad stood there, awkward, trying to make conversation with the Governor and First Lady, and left fifteen minutes after we arrived. The plan had been for us to walk the campus and have lunch, but that never happened...they were long gone. Truth be told, they never really liked being around me anyway. Actually, after that day we seldom spoke. On school breaks and summer I was giving permission to remain on campus so I could work.

"As part of my scholarship I had to work at the library, and for me it was the perfect job. Mr. Bowen treated all his staff equally and kept it quiet that I was on a scholarship. When I had a test, he let me study, and when I had nothing to do I would cover for him. Eventually I had a key and would open and close the library when he had something else going on. To be truthful after a while I hardly ever saw him. And that's why he was the best boss ever!"

"Didn't you meet Nick at the library?"

"Yes. He came looking for a book and couldn't find it. What a freaking moron. He was in his sophomore year studying law and he couldn't find a book? He was a dopey dope if I ever saw one. I had to practically take his hand and walk him over to the stacks. Then he came back the next few days later looking for a different book and asked me out for drinks. We went out a few times but it was odd. You know, I was convinced he was gay! We had four or five dates and he never tried anything, not even a kiss. One evening I was running late and asked him to meet me at my dorm. He shows up and I find out he and Ruth are friends. Nick's dad is one of the Governor's private and very active donors. Brad's dad was also part of the Governor's staff. Crazy. From that point on the three of us - then the four of us - were always together."

"Even when you...how do I say this...needed to be alone?"

"How do you know about that? Do I want to know how you know? Never mind. How do you know so much about me? We've never met, have we?"

Changing the subject, Bredra asked, "How did you get started in senior housing?"

"After we got married I worked my way up to be an executive director. Nick had his own firm but also did some work for his dad. The company I worked for was looking for an attorney to help them with a lawsuit, so I told them about Nick. They asked if he had represented senior housing in any lawsuit, and I said sure. Well, his father Big Nick had... and they never asked for proof of whether Nick had.

"So, after they resolved the lawsuit, the owners decided they had had enough of senior housing and wanted to sell, and asked Nick to help with the sale. He and I had talked about buying a community, and here was our opportunity. With Big Nick's connections we secured financing from a bank, then we bought another community, and another, and well, you get it."

"You do know Big Nick was the only investor on the first round or so."

"Big Nick never said anything out loud, but I knew that was the only way someone was loaning us millions. I had always liked him and looked to him as a second father...although I knew he wasn't thrilled when Nick married me."

"He adores you and how much you love his son, but, he, as well as others, worries that you will eventually self-destruct."

"Seriously?"

"Yes."

Annie sat quiet for some time then looked up, "Will I?"

"Well, the possibility does exist, and both Nicks are justified in their thinking."

"Well that's a sad factoid."

"I will never lie to you, Annie."

"Great to hear that, but you could lie when the truth hurts."

"I know, Annie; we all want that."

"So?"

"That is up to you, young-un. You have some very tough decisions to make. But as you know, it has always been up to you. Did you know the three men in your life, Big Nick, Nick, and the Governor all had a discussion about the topic of your self destruction on your wedding day? They came to a...how do I word it...an accord."

"No, I didn't know that. What did they talk

about?"

"Well," Bredra began, "the three men were sitting outside the church on a picnic table. Big Nick looked Nick square in the eyes. 'Son, make sure you really want to do this...you know that girl has a very dark side....' "

Nick was shocked his father even knew about her temper. "Why do you say that, Dad?"

"Nick, you had to know I did a background check on her, and have had my people keep an eye on her since you met just to make sure she doesn't hurt you, unintentionally of course."

Governor Wentz chuckled.

"Dad, I love her more than life itself. I love her as deeply as you love mom. I've learned from your example, Dad."

"Son, marriage is forever. Just make sure you are in this for the right reason."

"You're right, Dad, you caught me. I am marrying her for her money...I think she has about $10,000 in the bank."

Governor Wentz said quietly, "Well, a bit less than that." Both men looked over at him, shocked. "Hey, my Ruthie is part of this out-of-control freight train. My wife Julia loves her like a second daughter so I have to keep my eye on her. And I also agree there is a dark side; even Julia sees it and trust me, she only sees the best in people."

"Listen, thank you for your concern. I am taking

this conversation as both of you saying 'I love you.' I have seen her in her darkest moments and in her greatest light. Will it be a challenge married to her? Yes, but I see her as she can be. And the true Annie is a wonderfully loving, deeply committed, courageous woman and I'm at peace with marrying her. I have this," holding his hand up as Big Nick started to interrupt. "But, if I run into trouble of any kind, I promise to call you both and ask for help. Promise."

"Thank you, son."

"Thank you, Nick. Please know I'm always here for you."

"I know."

"Nick," the Governor added, "although I share your father's deep concern, I have also seen the way Annie protects Ruthie. During my re-election, if you remember, it got very dirty and a so-called friend of Ruthie's was going to give a very unflattering interview on TV about the family. Annie found out and had a chat with the girl. By the time my office heard about the interview and could intervene, the girl had cancelled the interview and dropped out of school. This is a roundabout way of saying that when it comes to Annie I am sure of one thing: if you are her friend, or husband, she will be loyal to the death. Cross her and, well, good luck. I also know, Nick, she loves you to the end of the earth...but please, my friend, don't forget that other side lurks within."

"Governor," Nick started to reply but the church door opened. It was Brad. "Nick, it's time, brother, let's get this going. There's cold beer on ice at the reception so please talk fast."

Chapter 10

Bredra stood up. "Let's grab an iced tea. I see there is much work to be done here."

Annie glanced at her watch but it had stopped at 11:11 a.m. "Damn, I left my phone at the house again."

"That's OK, no one is looking for you."

"You would know that with your super spidey sense?"

"You could say spidey sense, I prefer intuition."

"You're killing me."

"You have the same gift, missy, but your gift is much more powerful."

"If I was an intuitive or had any powers at all I can assure you my life would have been much different and much better."

"Sadly that's not true. That wasn't the path you accepted to walk before birth. Annie, see, you're a teacher, and spiritual teachers have a harder path to walk. However, keep in mind you accepted this path." She could tell Annie was lost.

"Let me start at the beginning. Before you are sent here to incarnate on earth, you are brought to the Great Hall and told what will take place while you are here. In fact, everyone who you have met in this life you knew before this life, and will know again in perhaps the next life. Your path was explained, exactly all that would unfold while you were here, and you still accepted it."

"Was I drunk?"

"Very funny, Annie...but this is serious stuff. Now take a moment and think, if you accepted this life, if you knew what was going to happen, and you still said yes, doesn't that make you feel better? Perhaps gives you your power back?"

"I have to think about that," Annie responded softly.

"Fair. You were also told about the Guardians and that you would be protected while you were here. But...and this is the big 'but'...when you draw your first breath here on this earthly plane you forget. All humans forget what they were told."

"Well that's bullshit...why forget?"

"It's how it works, but I have asked the same question, many times."

"So you mean the asshole who hurt me this time, I knew and liked before?"

"Yes. And during your next visit here, you may hurt him. But, as I understand, Lightworkers such as yourself don't come back very often. And no, I don't know why, I just know that is how I have been told it works."

"OK, I am with you so far."

"Do you remember meeting Gilhildafish? She was a guardian sent to protect you to help you begin your spiritual journey."

Annie sat thinking, wracking her brain, then it hit her. "Oh my God, when I was eleven...sitting outside with my dog. I have to admit for the longest time I thought she was a dream."

"We know. You were so sad. Remember, a few weeks before you were pushed down in the school yard by that girl who bullied you and you chipped your front teeth."

"She thought I was slow because I couldn't say my 'r' or my 's'. Wonder what ever happened to her?"

"Do you really care?"

"I do."

"She grew up, is a doctor, actually a pediatrician."

"I'm glad for her! But back to Gilhildafish. She said all would be well."

"Weren't you contemplating taking some of your mom's pills to end your life?"

"I forgot about that; it seems like a lifetime ago. Yes. She told me if I could hang in until I was eighteen everything would start to turn around for me. She made me promise her.

"And she promised to send Guardians to keep an eye out for me," Annie whispered. "I completely forgot."

"Do you know about the Law of Synchronicity?"

"Everything is synced up?"

"Close...there are Spiritual Laws that guide our lives, and when you know and use them correctly, wonderfully amazing things will start to happen."

"Like the Law of Attraction?"

"Now it's my turn to say good grief! Why is that the only law people know? Don't answer; yes, I know the book. Great book, but trust me, there are many other laws. Anyway, the Law of Synchronicity is just what it sounds like. The Universe, Spirit to be exact, places things in your path in a certain order, so if something bad arises Spirit knows whether to interfere or let it go.

"Let me give you a really quick example. While you were in college, after work one evening you were heading to a party and needed gas. You stopped at the station on the corner, got out of your car and noticed a car pulled up next to you. An older man got out and walked towards you."

"Yeah, yeah. There was something creepy about him; I jumped back into my car and drove to a different station."

"That is Synchronicity. The Guardians were synchronized to be there and tell you to run. If you had ignored them, and with free will you have the right to do so, you would not be here today."

"Seriously?"

"Yes, but other times the Guardians think it's funny not to help."

"Like...?"

"Remember a few years ago, when you and Ruth were staying in the penthouse of that hotel? You put your room service tray in the hallway and the door closed behind you. Ruth was sleeping."

"Damn it, yes. I pounded and pounded on the door, no answer. I had to do the walk of shame down thirty-seven floors to the lobby to get a key. Then the damn security guard had to escort me back so I could prove who I was. I asked him how many people in hotel robes try to break into the penthouse! He just stared at me."

"Well, you did keep calling him Barney Fife!"

"Then Ruth comes to the door in her goofy-ass PJs and yells at me for calling him Barney Fife and being rude to him. I was so mad I couldn't even talk to her."

"Your Guardians found it so darn funny watching you, we almost peed our pants. You were so mad standing in that hotel robe with no shoes and a golf hat. To this day it is a priceless memory."

Annie was laughing so hard at the visual image she could barely utter the words, "Screw you."

"What's the line in that movie? We've been watching you! OK, it's time to stretch our legs and walk some more." Bredra was already putting on her flip-flops.

"Let me grab a drink first." Leaning down to open the bar refrigerator, Annie started digging through it, setting beers on the counter until she found what she was looking for. Standing up, victorious, she had a bottle of Diet Coke in her hand. "Want one?"

"Sure, I haven't had a Diet Coke in years."

"Wish I could say the same, but I do drink more than my share. The kids are always on me about it. Kind of funny now that I think about it."

"What's that?"

"I drink copious amounts of alcohol, they don't say a word - but Diet Coke and they go on and on."

"I'm sure they've been introduced to your legendary temper."

"Ahh, that makes me sad but yes I know they have." Annie made a mental note to change that attitude and apologize to the kids.

Chapter 11

Brad and Ruth were sitting on the balcony of the penthouse at the hotel they now owned. Brad had been staring into space, and looked over at Ruth. "I think this could be the first day in very long time you haven't spoken to Annie."

"The day is still young," Ruth replied with a grin on her face.

Ruth adored Annie's bigger-than-life personality, where she herself was much more reserved. Ruth had loved college but for Annie it just was a box to check off her list. Ruth was valedictorian in high school and strove to maintain a 4.0 average. Annie was ecstatic to maintain a C average so she wouldn't lose her scholarship. Ruth was not a drinker at all and Annie loved to party. Most of the time the two of them would spend time together just hanging out with friends and having a few drinks. Ruth would nurse her glass of wine and laugh all night long at some of Annie's antics. They were just too darn funny.

Until "Dark Annie" would appear. Dark Annie drank crazy amounts of alcohol, took any drug she could get her hands on, spent the night who knew where, and then showed up at home the next morning, changed for work or class, and then would do it all again the next night. Never saying a word. Never talking about it.

Then, as abruptly as the behavior started, it would end. Annie was able to keep Dark Annie somewhat contained as she grew older, but Ruth knew there were times she sat in her hotel room and drank until she passed out. They never talked about it, any of it. But Ruth knew.

Now, turning to Brad she said, "There is a heavy sadness in Annie's soul. She can't always keep the inner monsters at bay. Don't judge. Remember, your life and for sure my life have been easy compared hers."

"Hey now, I worked hard to become a lawyer." Brad waited for Ruth to say something more or add to that comment, but it just hung over the table. Any discussion about Annie usually started and ended that way, ever since the day Nick introduced Brad to Ruth and Brad was sure it would never change. Ruth would defend Annie regardless of what she had done.

Brad continued thinking out loud, "I wonder if Nick knows? He must. I should ask him. It could be like 'Hey Nick, your wife seems to have a whole lot of crazy locked up...can you tell me why?' That would go over well, I'm sure."

Ruth didn't say anything, just sipped her wine and smiled. Brad knew there was a reason for her strong defense of Annie, but it was a secret that the two of them shared and Ruth was not telling. She knew where the darkness came from, but never spoke about it. Not since that night long ago in college.

"I think this weekend at Mike's place will be good for her."

"I heard you and Mike talking about it on the phone. Magical? Life changing? I think for her it had better include a ton of alcohol and work to keep her busy. I don't think I have ever seen her just sit and relax. The Governor and your mother especially loved her. I don't get that. Your mom would visit just to have lunch with her. That's crazy! They could not have been more opposite yet they were best buddies."

"I know. My mom did enjoy talking with her. You know what they say...opposites attract. Brad, name one person who doesn't like Annie."

Brad got up from the chair shaking his head. "I'm going to grab another bottle of wine. Do you want anything, my love?"

"No."

"Ruthie, you do have a deep profound love for her, and I love you, so my job is to protect you so she never hurts you."

"Brad, she is not capable of that - she has a gentle soul. But Annie had a much harder path than most. And like Humpty Dumpty I will help her keep the pieces together, and in some cases help her put them back together."

Chapter 12

"What time is it?" Annie asked Bredra as the sun starting sinking behind the surf.

"Must be around 8-ish. Annie, you know, for you to heal, my friend, you must know your Why."

"What?"

"Your Why."

"Why what?"

"Why it happened."

Annie looked at Bredra for what seemed like forever, never breaking eye contact. "I don't know what you mean," Annie said in a monotone voice. She turned around, picked up the book she had found, set a $10 bill on the cash register, looked one more time at Bredra, and opened the door.

"Annie, when you find your Why and heal it, your gift will be peace."

"Bredra, I have all I want and need. Plus if I find something else I need I'll buy it. Being rich affords me that luxury. I drink because I enjoy it."

"Keep telling yourself that, young-un."

Walking out the door, Annie stopped and turned around, looked Bredra in the eye, and said "Bredra, you don't know what you think you know. And I don't think I will ever find true peace...." And she let the door close behind her.

Chapter 13

Back at Mike's, Annie sat in the water, feeling the surf wash over her legs. The salt water hurt her knee but felt comforting at the same time. Annie reflected that she often seemed most comfortable when she was in pain, probably because for much of her childhood it was all she had known.

That thought made Annie start to cry...cry so hard she was shaking, while feeling every hurt, every pain she had ever experienced as a child. It seemed as if the pain was actually pouring out of her pores. She stared at the moon, asking - no, begging - the full moon to help stop the pain.

Annie couldn't remember the last time she had cried, but knew it had been a long time, most likely when Julia had died. Annie prided herself on never allowing her emotions to control her or to be shown to others. Emotions were a sign of weakness, and she promised herself when she left home never to be weak again. That thought made her start crying inconsolably again.

She sat there crying and drinking, a pattern she knew all too well. After way too many shots of vodka and an entire bottle of wine, Annie stumbled to bed, praying she would just pass out and forget. *"PLEASE GOD let me forget."* The tears came again.

"Mom, can I please go with you and dad?" Annie asked her mother for the umpteenth time.

"No honey, you stay home, Bobbie will watch you. We'll be home early."

"Mom, please *let me go.*"

"Stop whining like a little baby. You guys will have dinner and watch TV, and then please go to bed early." Her mother grabbed her coat, kissed Annie on the cheek and turned to Bobbie. "Take good care of your sister, Bobbie."

"Will do, mom, you know I always do."

Their father smiled and slapped Bobbie on the back. "You are the perfect son," he said, slipping him $20 for babysitting.

Annie heard the car drive down the street and…it started.

"Get naked, you little slut. You disgusting fat pig."

Sobbing, Annie took off her clothes. "Please don't hurt me, please don't."

"Oh, I won't leave a mark." He opened the back door. Their snow-covered backyard butted up against a wooded area; Annie was petrified of the woods. Her brother told her evil people who ate kids lived there and she better stay out of them unless he took her back there. He kicked her outside, pushed her into a snowdrift, held her face into the snow and slapped her ass. "Someday I'm going to fuck that, you little piece of shit slut. You are a dirty disgusting pig. No one will ever want you; you better be glad I am willing to take care of you." He slammed the door shut and turned off the light.

Annie knew that all she could do was stand naked, sobbing until he let her in. "Bobbie, please, it's freezing out here."

Bobbie was 5 years older than Annie. His parents had worked for Annie's dad but had been murdered, and because there was no one to take him in Annie's parents volunteered to raise him. Bobbie had behavior issues earlier in school but nothing too remarkable, and Annie's parents were proud of him. He played football and basketball, and was especially popular with the girls.

Bobbie finally yelled out the door, "If I let you in, piggy, will you squeal for me?"

That made Annie cry harder. "Bobbie, that hurts me so bad."

"Then freeze to death."

"OK, I will squeal for you."

Bobbie opened the door and Annie had to crawl in on hands and knees like a dog. Bobbie got behind her with his hard cock and rubbed it against her. She had to squeal like a pig until he flipped her over. "I think you're finally old enough." *After trying to penetrate her with no success, he pushed her mouth onto his penis and made her keep it there until he was satisfied.*

"Tell me you love that."

Sobbing, Annie weakly said, "I love it, Bobbie."

All of a sudden he yelled at her, "Get up, you disgusting slut...look what you made me do to you. Why do you make me do this? Go sit down for dinner." *As she stood up, Bobbie spat on her.* "Never mind, go to your room. you don't deserve dinner... you disgust me. You are so fucking fat, and if you tell Mom or Dad I'll tell them you're a liar. You know they love me better than you. Hell, Dad gave me $20 to do you."

Because Annie was only ten years old, she believed him. Once a month on Saturday her parents went out, and once a month Annie was tortured. The torture became worse and the sex became much harsher and painful. There was nothing she could do.

Annie woke up screaming, "Get off me! You're hurting me! Please...stop." She looked around the bedroom and cried, "What's wrong with me? Why can't I get those visions out of my head?" She whispered, "Please, dear God, help me, please." Annie had had dreams like this since the first time the abuse started. No matter how much she drank she couldn't stop the dreams...or the memories.

"Annie! Annie, it's OK. No one can hurt you anymore. I'm here with you. You will be fine. You will heal, I promise!"

Annie jumped up, looking around the room. "What or who the fuck was that?" Annie said trying to figure out where that voice came from. "Maria, is that you? Who said that?" She called out but there was no one there. The clock read 5:40 a.m. Annie sat there crying until she felt there could be nothing left inside. Finally, she dragged herself out of bed and went outside where, sitting back in the sands, she cried and cried some more. After she was totally cried out, Annie went in to take a shower, hoping that would make her feel better.

While in the shower, Annie heard someone say, "I'm here, waiting for you."

"Who?" Then, she knew.

Jumping out of the shower, she threw on a pair of blue shorts and a baggy white tank top. With no makeup or jewelry, she pulled her hair back in a ponytail and, carrying her flip flops, she walked to the bookstore. As she opened the door, she heard Bredra say, "Annie, dear, I'm outside."

Walking out on the patio, the mist from the ocean felt like a loving hand wrapping around Annie's body. She felt at home.

"Rough night?"

"Extremely."

"You had to see it."

"Why? *Seriously*? You sit here and tell me I had to see it? *I fucking lived it!* Don't you get that? Don't you understand that concept? I have no desire to look at it. Because in case you missed the fucking memo, I lived it!"

"Have you ever told anyone what really happened to you?"

"Ruth, kind of, and Nick, kind of. Ruth knows more than Nick."

"Why not tell them the whole story?"

"What purpose would that serve?"

"You have to talk to someone. You need to process it to understand."

"I've processed it."

"Annie, I can promise you one thing."

"What?"

"None of what happened was ever your fault."

"On an intellectual level I completely understand that but...." Her voice trailed off and she started softly crying.

"This is why you drink so much, trying to escape."

"I know," Annie whispered back. "I just try to mute the voices, the memories. It never leaves me, Bre. Doesn't matter what I do, it's always there. That is what's so hard. The memories. I can't escape the damn memories. So yes, that's why I drink, for fuck's sake. To mute the memories, make myself feel better, to be healed for that short period of time."

"Does it work?"

"No," Annie started crying again. "Doesn't matter how fast I run, how hard I work or how much I drink, it's there."

"Annie, just start with this...you are here, exactly where you are."

"Bredra, will the pain go away?"

"No."

"It's always there simmering."

"I know."

"I'm so bone tired."

"I know."

"I'm so tired of the battle that's raging within."

"I know."

"I always feel like I'm losing."

"I know."

"Well that's eff-ing helpful, my Shaman friend."

"Young-un, if you were to forget what happened, there would be no sense, no purpose for the event to have occurred in the first place."

"That would be fine with me."

"Do you think Spirit placed you here to suffer? For no reason?"

"Yes."

"So Annie, in this most powerful universe where we are all interconnected, people are supposed to suffer for no reason?"

"Yes."

"Annie, there is a reason for all and all has a reason. Otherwise what would be the sense to the suffering?"

"Bingo. First thing you said that we agree on…what is the sense?"

"There is always a reason."

"So I have to find the sense, the reason for all of this? That's bullshit!"

"Your purpose will be illuminated. Every event has a reason, a Why. Learn the reason, understand the event."

"So, keeping with your line of thought, throwing out the trash has a reason," Annie said disgusted.

"Yes. Perhaps it's the act of walking outside, or the act of helping the environment. What's important is the meaning you place on the act, the event! For you, it's the meaning you placed on the abuse or how you chose to interpret the abuse."

"So you're saying change the meaning, change the emotion?"

"Change what it means to you in this minute. Reframing the meaning takes away the power of the event. You can reframe your memories to make them easier to live with."

"Will it change them overnight?"

"Change is not a video game - you don't get to skip a level."

"So, I won't forget."

"No, but you can change the power of the memory."

"Hmmm."

"You must, you have to know it wasn't your fault. It was the destiny you chose."

"Whatever."

"Understand young-un, you have complete dominion over *you*. Most people fear the answer, or fear that the answer they find can't be true because it sounds too easy. Don't want to get their hopes up. They believe they can't change the meaning. But the choice has always been yours to make! The power to change is there in you; you just need to do the work."

"That is?"

"To find your answer to Why. You first have to understand the event then find your gift hidden in the Why of it. You own this life, so own the experiences and the meaning you give it. You and you alone control the meaning you place on the abuse."

They sat in silence for some time watching seagulls dive into the ocean for their dinner.

"Let's try looking at this a different way. Annie, what is your gift?"

"Making money."

"No, your true gift, the 'why you are here' gift."

"To make money."

"Funny. What is your true gift?"

"Business."

"No, Annie. You have a much deeper purpose, otherwise the past would be for naught."

"I'm listening."

"Remember when we first met I told you that you signed up for this before you were even born?"

"Yes."

"So if you chose this path would it not make sense there has to be a reason, a greater purpose? Don't you think?"

"Not really. Why in God's name would anyone want to go through this pain? So, Bredra, what? What's the purpose?"

"Annie, think. When you look at people using your intuition, or as you call it, spidey sense, what do you see?"

"I just see them."

"Think deeper. When you are meeting people, 'sizing them up' as you say, what do you see?"

"I see people as they *could* be, keeping in mind that some are how they *should* be."

"Exactly. So are you where you could be or where you should be?"

"Bredra, I don't know...I'm so broken I will never be fixed."

Bredra stood up, pointing her finger at Annie. "BULLSHIT!"

Annie jumped. "Bredra, did you just say a bad word? Hell, I didn't think you knew any."

"I know my share, just don't feel the need to use them. Not very ladylike."

"Good grief...Julia Jr.!"

"Annie, thinking you are broken is your first

mistake. NEVER think that way. You are not broken; no one is broken. As humans you are who you are. You are a perfect being living a human experience. Yet people run around trying to fix themselves, looking for a quick fix to make themselves feel better. Seeking advice from a stranger. As if a stranger can tell you something you don't already know! Then, these same people believe what they are told and they think they are healed. Oh, until they start on the hamster wheel of drinking again, sleeping around, doing anything they can to feel better."

Annie leaned forward, listening. "But," Bredra continued, "What you're really doing is just punishing yourself, over and over again. Letting the memories win. Or another way to say it...letting your abuser win while keeping yourself in pain. Punishing you. A million tiny cuts over and over, each and every day. Then you get mad at yourself, beat yourself up, drink, feel better and then start the whole pattern over. Annie, *you chose this life, this path*! Let that sink in. Let that empower you. If you chose this destiny, then how can it hurt you?"

"I did? No, I mean...I DID! I DID! I DID!" Annie was screaming at the top of her lungs. "I did! And if I chose it here must be a grander reason, right? So my gift is...? I got nothing."

"Annie, do you remember the seven-steps thing you developed? What happened to that?"

"The what?" Annie asked perplexed, "the seven steps to WTF? No idea."

"OK."

They sat in silence, listening to the surf come in, slapping against the barrier wall. The waves were hypnotic.

"When I'm here, I'm so at peace, Bredra."

"I know, young-un."

"Oh my God, Bre! I just remembered that seven step presentation. I wrote that years ago for some crazy seminar I was asked to give. It was a personal development seminar, and they wanted me to talk about women overcoming their challenges. How I overcame my challenge of, according to them, being poor and rising up. I think I called it 'Seven Steps to Find Your Why and Transform Your Life.' It was a great presentation, if I must say. The reception to it was amazing...I received letters for a few years after from people telling me how much it helped change their life. Of course, looking back, a hell of a lot of good that it did for me. Well, you know...that's not true. Those steps did help me to get some of my life together, at least hold it together."

"Was it a quick fix?"

"There is no such thing as a quick fix, Bredra."

"Well learned!"

"No, this is not even close. To make changes you have to know Why, but once you know Why the rest is a tad bit easier. Right?"

"Annie, do you know yet the answer to those two questions I asked you last week?"

"Wow...that was only a few days ago but seems like a lifetime."

"In some ways, Annie, it was," Bredra laughed.

"The answer to why haven't I secured financials for the package of communities is easy to know, but hard to admit. That part of my journey is over; it's Nickolas's turn. I've done all I can. Well no, that's not true...I should say I've done all I *want* to do. Time for me to exit stage right.

"And number two was my Why. Well," Annie sat thinking about it. "My Why, as in Why did I choose this path? You know, I've had a great life. Made money, built a great business that has done much good for our seniors, great education, great family and friends, and yet I am a functioning alcoholic running from demons. My WHY? I don't think it has been shown to me. If I was to guess, keeping with the theme of that personal development seminar I did, it's my story of overcoming and redemption. That the Universe is here to support us if we stay present and listen. Maybe it's showing people how to find their Gift hidden in their Why. But I'm not there yet."

"Ah, but you're on the right path, young-un."

"Can I get back to you on my Why?"

"Absolutely. Annie, we're done here. Now it's up to you to...how does Ruth put it? Time for you to put Humpty Dumpty back together."

"I know. It's long overdue."

"No, Annie. This Universe works on perfect timing, so now is the perfect time. The time you are ready and prepared to figure it out."

"Hey, I have an idea."

"What?"

"Let's meet back here in exactly 3 months and I'll have my Why, then."

"Deal."

As Annie was leaning over to get her shoes she reminded Bredra, "I am still going to be here tomorrow so I'll stop by with muffins at 10:00 sharp."

Bredra was laughing as Annie closed the door behind her.

Chapter 14

"Maria must have been here again," Annie thought, walking into the kitchen. She leaned over to grab her ringing phone. It was Nick but she was not fast enough so the call went to voicemail. As she set the phone down, it rang again.

"Hello?"

"Hi honey, how are you doing?"

"I'm fine, Nick...I just need to do some thinking...well, a lot of thinking. I just spent the day at the bookstore talking with the owner, and I don't how she does it but that woman knows things about me that *I* didn't know. Nick, I have so much to figure out. I have to figure *me* out and my future."

Nick sat silent a minute or two. "I love you to the end of the earth. I told you when we got married that I would and will do anything to protect you. Do anything to help you. I will always make sure no one ever, ever hurts you."

"I know Nick and I love you so much. I have also put you through a lot and you've never asked and instead stood patiently by. And at this moment there's nothing you can do. I need to figure this stuff out."

"Annie, my love, I'm here for you."

"I want to go away."

"I will send the plane."

"Isn't it being repaired?"

"Oh yeah, I forgot, but I think we can afford to rent a plane."

"Drop the story. I know the plane is fine! You all just needed to trap me here, and to that I say...thank you!"

"I'll call the pilot, tell him wheels up."

"I kind of thought you would be the pilot and pick me up. Ruth said we could use her island. Hey, you know what's funny? If you'd told ten-year-old Annie she would have a friend that actually owned an island I would have laughed until I wet my pants."

"Are you sure you want me to go with you?"

"Of course I do, you're my guy. I'm your girl."

"I'll be there at first light."

"I can't wait to see you. I love you so much, Nick."

"And I you." Nick said as he hung up.

There was one more call Annie had to make. She picked up the phone and dialed.

Ruth answered.

"Hi, what's up, what's wrong?"

"You know, you're the second person who asked me that today." Annie said before falling quiet.

"Annie, are you there? Hellloooo? Where did you go?"

In barely a whisper, Annie asked, "You know, don't you?"

Ruth was silent, unsure what to say. She knew exactly what Annie was asking and had been worried this day would arrive. Ruth remembered what her mother had told her a long time ago: "Never lie to her; she has to know she can trust you."

"Yes, honey, I know. You told me back in our freshman year."

"I'm sorry; I should never have burdened you with that secret."

"It was not a burden, Annie...hey, I can be there

in a few hours."

"No. Ruth this is something I have to figure out. I have to look at it for the first time and process it."

There was a long pause.

"Ruth, thank you for keeping the secret. You are now free to release it if you feel it will help." Annie started laughing, "I'm sure Brad would love to know."

"Annie..."

Annie interrupted, "Seriously, Ruth, you want me to believe Brad never asked you about me? Hell, he asked Nick a couple times."

"He did not!"

"He did indeed; ask him, my friend."

"I'll kill him. Annie, it has always been your story to tell, not mine."

"Ruth, I love you. Thanks for keeping Humpty Dumpty together...now I have to figure things out myself."

"I love you, Annie, and can be there in a few hours."

"No, but thanks. Nick is on his way; we are going to your island!"

Ruth chuckled. "I'll send the codes to you. Brad and I came home yesterday so the island is all yours. Call me if you need anything. You know, Annie, since the first day we met at college we've talked every day, including when we were both on our honeymoons and you were birthing babies."

Laughing, Annie responded, "You're right. I remember, I was heading in for a C-section and called to tell you to follow up on that one acquisition. Nick was so mad at me. Wow! We'll talk soon, promise. I just need to exit stage right and find me. I'm not sure I know who I really am."

"I love you, Annie."

"Ruth, you are my soul sister and I will be forever grateful for your friendship. I have never said thank you. Thank you for always being there, for always picking up the pieces that you call Humpty Dumpty. I promise you I'm going to do better. I will get this under control. You know, Mike is right. That bookstore is magical. I'll tell you more when I see you.

"We have a lot to talk about, but right now I need to just think. This is a journey I have to walk alone and with Nick. I think I have to tell him about my childhood...what happened. But Ruth, I'll be OK. For the first time ever in my life I feel like I really will be OK."

Brad walked in as Ruth was hanging up the phone. "Are you all right?"

Ruth was smiling, "I think she's starting to heal. I think she's going to uncover whatever demons are chasing her. She's finally willing to look within to figure this out."

Brad held her hand. "You are the best friend you could ever have been. You know most people would've left by now."

"Brad," Ruth said, "this is the path I picked. I knew the first day I met Annie standing on the doorway of our dorm room, looking both totally out of place and exactly where she belonged at the same time. Definitely a gift of hers - she can fit in anywhere at any time. You know I've never told anyone this, but when my father decided to run for re-election as Governor I thought I should get a different roommate. I worried about what she might do that could impact my father's campaign. Can you believe that?"

Brad laughed. "Actually I can. I was surprised when we first met that you were friends with her. Especially after I met your first boyfriend, Reginald Master, Jr. What a tight-ass he was. What changed your mind?"

"There was one weekend we were at a bar and she got really drunk."

"What's new?"

"Be nice, Brad. On the drive home she told me a story. The weird thing was I knew when she started telling the story that I had heard it before a long time ago. I also knew at that exact moment what I was always meant to do…to help walk her through her journey. And that's what I've done."

"You've done that a million times over."

"Thanks."

"Hey, what was the story?"

"She just told me that you actually asked Nick about it a couple of times."

"Me?"

"Yes, you. I should be mad at you. Brad, to be honest, if I told you, you would be horrified. It's a story that still haunts me and I didn't actually live it. I totally understand what it must do to her to have lived through that."

"Ruth, we all know something terrible happened to her. We had guessed it involved abuse but out of respect to her none of us ever asked. I knew that Nick knew, however."

"He does but only small parts. Like me. We only know snippets, and believe me that's all I ever want to know. I'm sure Nick feels the same way. It's Annie's burden to carry, and hers to share."

Brad gave Ruth a bear hug, kissing her deeply, then looked into her stunningly blue eyes. "This is why I fell in love with you. You are the most compassionate, loving elitist I will ever meet."

Ruth glared at Brad until they both cracked up. "I love you too."

Chapter 15

The next morning, Annie jumped out of bed, dressed quickly and headed towards the store. *"I need to say goodbye. I have to tell her last night was the first night in forever that I didn't have a drink. Hell, I didn't even want a drink. I feel so happy, so alive!"* Getting closer to the store Annie stopped dead in her tracks. There was no need to her to go any further.

Annie knew the store was closed.

As it had to be.

The plane touched down at the Blue Rose airport and Annie was so excited she could barely wait to get off the plane.

"I can't wait to see Bredra!"

Nick cleared his throat, "Annie, this is your 'coming out of 3 months of seclusion' party so I took the liberty of inviting some folks."

"Well, that explains a tarmac filled with Leer jets. Who?"

"The kids, of course."

"Of course."

"Ruth, Brad, and Mike. I never could reach Bredra, but her daughter Megan will be there as well. I can't wait to meet Bredra."

"Me either, plus I have so much to tell her. To ask her."

Walking up to the bookstore, Nick took Annie's hand. "Don't be nervous."

"How can you tell I'm nervous? You've always seemed to know."

"You have a tell - it's hard to notice, but there's a tell," Nick laughed.

"What?"

"I probably shouldn't tell you, but you tap your index finger."

"Really. Hmmmmm."

"Annie?"

"Yes, my love."

"You look fantastic." Annie was wearing a form fitting, white silk dress, the five carat diamond necklace Nick had surprised her with last night with matching earrings and bracelet, and red Jimmy Choo heels. She had pulled her hair back into a ponytail. "She never does that in public," Mike thought. "My lady is changing."

"What are you staring at?"

"You, baby. Let's blow this off and go hang out on the beach."

Annie started laughing as she opened the door of the bookstore.

"Annie!" Ruth screamed, running over to hug her.

"Mom!" Emma shouted. Soon everyone was hugging, laughing, all trying to talk at the same time. Even Kevin and Tim were hugging her.

"Before the guest of honor arrives I have a few things to say..." Annie began.

"What a shocker." Nickolas yelled out.

"First, thank you. I have been, over the years, an ass, treating some of you not very nicely. Thank you for always being there for me and for loving me. Second…Nickolas, I need to confess. I was offered financing on three different occasions and turned it down. I'm sorry, son."

"Mom, Mom," Nickolas raised his hand to stop her, "Mom, I know."

"How?"

"Every time you turned someone down they would call me and try to do an end run. Each time I told them because of that we would never do business with them. I explained to them we are family first. Of course they said I would regret it, but I knew I never would. I told them that my mom is the best business woman and greatest mother ever. I said, 'This is HER company, not mine. If she wants to stay at fifteen properties, that's where we'll stay.'"

"Nickolas, that is where you are wrong."

"What? You *are* a great business woman and mom."

"Oh, I agree with that." Everyone laughed. "But it's your company now. After talking with my partners, your father and Ruth, I've decided to retire. Emma and you will share ownership. Your father and I have made our money, many times over. It's time for us to see what the future holds."

Nickolas's eyes got misty. "Thanks, Mom."

"I love you, Mom." Emma walked over and hugged her. "You won't regret this."

Blue Rose Bookstore: the Gift of Why

"If I were you the first thing I would do is walk over there and ask Mike to honor his deal." Annie looked over everyone's heads. "Where's Bredra?"

"Hi Annie!" A woman in her mid-forties walked over. She wore light brown capri pants with a white blouse tied at her waist. She was a little on the heavy side, with short curly jet black hair, and looked exactly like her mother.

"You're Bredra's daughter, Megan!"

"Yes," Megan answered as they hugged.

"Where is the guest of honor? We made a deal to meet back here in three months."

Megan handed an envelope to Annie. The cursive handwriting spelled, "To Annie Walker."

"Mom asked me to make sure I handed this to you personally."

"She's not coming?"

"Annie, my Mom passed away many years ago."

Annie just stood there staring, with a confused look on her face. "What?" She started laughing hysterically. "Come on, where is she?"

Mike stepped forward, "Annie, she really is dead."

Tears welled up in Annie's eyes. Suddenly the room started spinning and grew dim. Annie looked over and saw Bredra sitting on the veranda, looking out at the ocean. She turned and waved Annie over, saying, "Let's talk."

"Bre?"

"Yes, young-un."

"I'm confused."

"Don't be; I am dead."

"How? Why?"

"Well, the why is easy - it was my time. The how was cancer."

"I'm sorry."

"Obviously, not as sorry as I. Anyway you're my replacement."

"Replacement? For what?"

"Teaching women to find their true meaning and purpose, their Why."

"Wait - beep beep, back up. What about Tim and the muffins? He asked me to bring the food over."

"If you remember, you asked *him*. I made arrangements before I passed that when people asked about the bookstore, Tim would give them a muffin and send them over. If they see me when they enter, as you did, they are ready to begin healing and remain. If they see nothing, they walk back to the coffee shop and tell Tim no one was there, and continue on their path. Foolproof...until recently, that is."

"Who else can see you here? Mike?"

"He can and still does see me."

"Megan?"

"Same as Mike."

"Look at them. Everyone else in the room is frozen in time, except them...they are chatting away. You see, only people who are spiritually attuned can see me."

Annie looked over, they both turned and waved.

"Wait, you said until recently? What happened?"

"The world is changing, Annie. There seems to be more unhappiness. People are growing unsure of themselves and not trusting the world around them, searching, trying to find answers. Sadly, they don't even know what the questions are, but they want answers. And in my present state...."

"Dead."

"Yes, dead...I can't keep up. More and more people feel broken, convinced that something is missing in their lives. I don't know the reason for this shift, but I need someone...how can I say this...*above ground* to help me. You were sent here to do that. You have the same gift as I, except, of course, your gift is much stronger. Annie, in your heart you know you're here to make a profound difference."

"What is that?"

"Remember in the Keynote speech you gave so long ago what your overarching theme was?"

"That you can't be fixed...because *you are not broken!* That if you can see it you can be it, so Ignite Your Possibilities."

"That's your message to the world, Annie!"

"More than that...it's my Why, Bre."

Bredra started laughing her deep belly laugh. "Well played, my friend. Continue with your Why...."

"So, if nobody is ever broken, I would rather show people their greatness...help them understand why they do what they do, and how that will take them to who they're meant to be. I won't focus on people being broken but rather who they could and should be.

"Working in senior housing, I've had the honor to meet and speak with countless seniors during my thirty-plus-year career. I learned one overarching message from these seniors. At least eighty percent of them said the same thing when reflecting on their lives: *'I wish I had taken more chances and dared to FOLLOW*

Blue Rose Bookstore: the Gift of Why

MY DREAMS, MY PASSIONS.' Each one of their statements began with 'I WISH...'."

"Annie, could this be your message to the world?" Bredra asked.

"Yes, as I told you before, I see people as they *could* be unless they are where they *should* be."

"Annie, you are being called. Are you going answer the call? Are you ready to be a Spiritual Teacher, my dear?"

As Annie was thinking about the significance of this conversation, she could hear the other guests talking. Suddenly she realized their voices were becoming louder and clearer. Annie glanced over at Mike, then back at Bredra, who was beginning to fade from Annie's vision. "Yes! I'm ready. After all, it's who I was born to be." Then just as suddenly, as Bredra disappeared the voices were all the same volume again.

Nick walked outside and looked at Annie, who asked, "What are you staring at?"

"You! You look radiant, my love. Let's walk down to the beach together and see what happens." Nick said, half joking.

"Swear to God, you are acting like we're back on the island."

"We could go back to the island."

Taking Nick's arm, Annie whispered, "Nick, I'm being called."

"I'm not sure what that means but if it's what you want then I want it for you as well."

"Let's go inside and read what's in the envelope."

Walking back into the bookstore, Annie looked down at the envelope still in her hand and slowly opened it. The letter was hand written on parchment paper.

"Annie Walker, welcome to the Blue Rose Bookstore. It is my intention that you carry on my legacy. Over my 20 years here at the bookstore I have been able to appear, to be seen and heard, to only those that were ready to change. If they were unable to see me they were not prepared to change."

Annie continued reading. "However, times are changing. The Universe is reaching a point where more people are starting to seek answers on their own and are open to change. To continue helping people figure out their Why and 'Find Their Blue Rose,' the Guardians know there needs to be a larger 'more alive' presence. Spiritual growth needs a positive person, a spiritual teacher, who understands the greatness of the human soul and, Annie Walker, that is you!

Tim, Kevin and Mike have agreed to continue assisting you but the rules may need to change because, well, people can actually see you. You may need a partner to help because, as you say, you are a talker. But I believe with all my heart and soul in you! If you need me you know how to reach me in the spiritual realm.

If you agree to accept this offer, the bookstore is yours for the price of $1.00. If you do not agree, Megan may sell the bookstore for fair market value.

Young-un, here's to...Discovering Your Gift of Why and Finding Your Blue Rose.

Love you,
Bredra."

It was so quiet in the room you could hear a fish jump in the ocean. Wiping tears from her eyes, Annie looked at Nick. "What do you think?"

"My love, I can work anywhere on this planet as long as we're together. If you're in, as always, I'm in."

"I love you, Nick."

"Oh brother, you guys are killing me…get a room!" Nickolas yelled to his parents.

Ruth locked eyes with Brad, who smiled and shook his head. "I know, I know."

"Annie?"

"Ruth?"

"I hear you may be looking for a partner. I think I can help finance the bookstore."

"Can you now? All fifty cents? Better be a cash offer!"

Everyone again burst out laughing.

"Hey, Nick?" Brad yelled. "I've always wanted to learn how to surf; how about you, old man?"

"Yesss, let's go get a surfboard!"

"Hey," Nickolas chimed in. "Me too!"

"Sorry, son," Nick Jr said. "You own a company now and it's time for you to follow your own dreams."

Annie listened to the conversations around her. Some were about the changes to the company but most about the changes to Annie.

Looking to the heavens, Annie whispered, "Bredra, thank you for saving me. For helping me heal. I understand I chose to walk the path of horrendous abuse so I can be an example to others in the world. To show them that anything is possible if they believe in themselves first. To teach that they have the ability to reframe and transform their life, and help them understand they chose this life. And to teach that healing is possible if they are willing."

Epilogue

Annie walked to the bookstore, glancing at the time on her phone and thinking about the call she just had. *"I need to pick up the pace."*

Ten minutes after arriving, the door opened, the bell rang and a woman entered.

"Hey, I told that guy across the street I was walking over to get a book. He asked me to deliver your takeout order like I'm a delivery person. What are you, some princess that can't walk your ass across the damn street and pick up your own food?"

"Hello Kyra, I've been waiting for you...."

Author's Final Words...

You are exactly where you are!

I have walked my path, gone on my journey. I walked the life laid out before me. I have the battle scars to prove that I have lived my life fully while also drinking from the nectar of the gods.

I have no regrets, only a heart filled with forgiveness and love.

I encourage you to embrace your journey because in the end, believe it or not - it was ALL YOUR CHOICE!

Karen Barno

Acknowledgements

Thank you to everyone who has made this book possible!

My life has been a magic carpet ride with no regrets. I drank from the nectar of the Gods and had a great time. My journey has been filled with soul crushing loses but way more soul lifting events.

Dennis, you're my guy, my little buddy, best husband ever for over 30 years! Your love and encouragement has helped this dreamer keep following my dreams. I would never have accomplished anything in my life without you by my side. I love you! You believed in me even when I was a train wreck.

Allex, you have always lived your truth. You've shown that when you have a dream, never let anything EVER stand in your way until you accomplish it. I am so proud that you're my daughter.

Nancy, I met you when I was born and you're still my best sister, the only sister, but still the best. I love having you as a best friend, hanging out with you…and Laguna Beach, here we come.

Crystal, here's to five years of you listening to me talk nonstop about this book. You have always encouraged and gently pushed me more than a few times to keep writing. For helping me with all my technology issues and doing speed proofing.

Aunt Jane, you have been my biggest cheerleader! I so appreciate all you have done for me!

Deedra, thank you for reminding me to turn on my inner light. To keep following my spiritual path and "all will be well." You were right... all is well.

Holly Matson of Lightseeds by Holly, my proofreader and editor, thank you for your patience and gift of the written word.

To all the guardians who pushed and continue to encourage me, never allowing me to quit or give up until I fulfill my destiny.

Life is to be enjoyed.
Listen to your inner voice - it will guide you well.

About the Author

Karen Barno is a catalyst for change, a retreat leader and an international motivational speaker.

Karen's motivation to coach women and help them find their true passion was born out of her own painful journey through a physically and verbally abusive childhood. She graduated at the very bottom of her high school class, joined the Air Force, and in the real world continued to struggle. She was not able to hold a job for more than 3 years and found it nearly impossible to erase the "I can't, I'm not worthy" beliefs from her consciousness.

After her personal journey of healing and transformation, Karen is now driven by a singular vision: to help women define their own success for their career and personal life, guide them beyond the fears and lead them toward actualizing their dreams. Karen has dedicated herself to providing resources for women to shorten their learning curve on the path of self-awareness. Through private mentoring and group training programs, Karen now teaches techniques to help women unlock their spiritual potential and nurture their health and happiness while embracing their unique talents that will ultimately change the world around them.

Karen is a certified Shaman, Reiki Master, and also holds a Bachelor's of Science in Business Management, and lives in Arizona with her husband, daughter and bulldog named Rosie. She is an avid golfer and loves to travel with her family.

To learn more about Karen's work, contact her at Karen@KarenBarno.com or Facebook.com/KarenBarno.

Coming soon!
A companion workbook for Blue Rose Bookstore!
Visit us online to watch for the release announcement.

www.KarenBarno.com

Made in the USA
San Bernardino, CA
16 February 2018